D1714496

IKIGAI FOR TEENS

Finding Your Reason for Being

HÉCTOR GARCÍA
& FRANCESC MIRALLES

SCHOLASTIC INC.

Library of Congress Cataloging-in-Publication Data available

ISBN 978-1-338-67083-7

1 2020

Printed in the U.S.A.   23
First edition, 2021

Book design by Baily Crawford

To Niko,
who will have great adventures
on the ikigai path.

CONTENTS

Preface:
A Mapless Journey

*"When the explorer is ready,
their path appears."*

FROM A ZEN PROVERB

It is no accident that this book is in your hands. It has come looking for you because you are ready to carry out a mission—the most fascinating journey of your life.

You are headed for a mysterious world, where you will sometimes wonder what to do or even feel lost, but it's worth carrying on because there's a great prize waiting for you at the end: Your reason for being.

It will be an exciting journey! You'll find clues along the way. Some of them will help. Others won't lead you anywhere. They are there to test you on your path and challenge your character and courage.

Just as there is no rose without a thorn, no great adventure is without its struggles and difficulties.

This journey has no map because the territory has not

been explored before. It is a brand-new world you alone can discover as you walk through it. And it is your own destiny—the place where you are going to find your future.

If you get tired of walking, you can ride a bike.

Imagine you're already sitting on that bike. The tires are full of air, the chain has been oiled, and you're pedaling easily along a flat path in the middle of the forest.

After biking for a long while, sweating with the sun at your back, you reach a point where the path forks—well, actually, it splits in four; from here on you can take one of the different paths. Each has a sign showing a destination.

Written on the first one in large golden letters is:

$$\boxed{\textbf{MONEY}}$$

Maybe you want to take this path for your life-changing journey. Don't they say money can buy anything? Or almost anything . . . It can't buy love, as the most famous band in the history of rock music once sang (that would be the Beatles, more than fifty years ago). It can't buy you friends, either. (Some people might say it's the other way around—if you're rolling in money, you'll always wonder if people want to get close to you so they can have some of it.)

Can happiness be bought? No, it cannot.

Before choosing to go down this path, it's worth checking out the other three. That way, you'll be able to make the best choice for you.

Let's take a look at the second one.

FAME

Maybe you've sometimes dreamed of being a celebrity. It must be awesome to get hundreds of thousands of likes every time you post a video, to have millions of followers on social media, to be asked for selfies everywhere you go. But what if it ends up being a nightmare? What if all you feel amid that craziness is intense loneliness?

Many pop stars say that, despite being onstage in front of thousands of people, after the shows they go home . . . alone.

Before choosing this path for your life, consider the two that are left. Here comes the third one:

POWER

It must be fun to be powerful. Superheroes always have some sort of special power that the rest of humanity doesn't (even if it's just turning ginormous and green and smashing stuff). Fantasy aside, a person with power is someone who has the fate of many others in their hands.

A queen holds such power over her subjects; a company boss wields it over their workers.

Powerful people are often more feared than loved—keep that in mind if you are thinking of taking this path.

Before deciding, though, you'll want to see the fourth and final sign at the intersection.

IKIGAI

What in the world does that mean? Don't worry—this book has fallen into your hands precisely so that you can find out.

Remember that imaginary bike you were riding when you came to the four paths? Get off it, take a break from the journey, and sit down someplace comfortable where you can catch your breath. It has been tough making it this far, right? You need to pause to think things over.

Before deciding on your destination, stop for a moment to ponder what you're about to read on the following pages . . .

WHAT DO I WANT TO DO WITH MY LIFE?

I.
The Ikigai Compass

"Being lost is good.
If you don't get lost,
you can't find yourself."

Many languages have words that don't have an exact translation into English, and one of them is *ikigai*.

In Japanese, it is written 生き甲斐 and is made up of two parts:

IKI 生き = LIFE
GAI 甲斐 = TO BE WORTHWHILE

In other words, the literal meaning of ikigai would be "a worthwhile life," although it is usually translated as "life goal"—that is, the mission that gives your life meaning.

Simply put, ikigai is the reason you get out of bed

in the morning—and not just because the alarm went off. It's like an internal motor, or a waking dream, that inspires you to start the day.

The nineteenth-century German philosopher Friedrich Nietzsche said: *"He who has a why to live for can bear almost any how."*

Imagine that your passion is mountain climbing and you're on vacation with your parents, or a field trip with your classmates in a national park with peaks of all sizes for you to conquer.

Maybe you didn't get any sleep the night before because it was too hot, or because you were being bitten by mosquitoes, or because people were up late, talking loudly in the cabin next door.

When dawn breaks, you feel *sooo* tired. You'd think it would be a major struggle to peel yourself off the mattress and plant two feet on the floor. But no, you actually leap out of bed with amazing ease, never mind your sleepless night. The surrounding mountains are there for you! And you can't wait to lace up your boots and start exploring them for yourself.

That's why you take a lightning-fast shower, wolf down a good breakfast, and set off to carry out your life mission—your ikigai. When you start out for the day's peak, all the tiredness and irritations of the night before suddenly disappear. The fresh air on your face is all you need to begin climbing up toward the summit like a champion.

All the unease is left behind because your ikigai is pulling you along, giving you the energy of a superhero.

There is an old saying that goes "in times of trouble, sing your troubles away"—as long as your passion is singing, that is. You might want to let your passion play the piano instead . . .

LANG LANG'S IKIGAI

Have you ever heard of Lang Lang? Today, he is considered to be one of the best pianists in the world. The story of a boy born in the northeast of China is proof of how far you can go if you follow your passion in life.

Although his father played the erhu, a traditional Chinese two-stringed instrument, Lang Lang would discover his instrument—and his ikigai—through *Tom and Jerry* cartoons. When he was only two years old, he saw "The Cat Concerto." And became completely obsessed.

In the seven-minute episode, the proud and jovial house cat, Tom, gives a piano recital in a packed concert hall. Jerry, the mouse, who was napping inside the piano, is suddenly shaken from his sleep and decides to get revenge against the cat, who simply wishes to carry on playing his music. One of the typical slapstick Tom-and-Jerry battles begins, in time to the orchestra's performance.

Young Lang Lang, though, was fascinated by something else. Apart from the brawl between the cat and the mouse, he was amazed by the piece of music that Jerry keeps playing in the midst of so many difficulties (*He who has a why . . . can bear almost any how.*); it was Franz Liszt's Hungarian Rhapsody no. 2.

It was the first time Lang Lang had ever heard Western classical music and, despite being only two years old, he felt compelled to learn the piano so that someday he, too, could play that marvelous piece.

Lang Lang had just discovered his ikigai.

At the age of three, he started to take piano lessons. At the age of five, he won a piano competition in his town and gave his first public recital.

However, he didn't meet with massive success. Not immediately. When he was nine, Lang Lang auditioned for Beijing's Central Conservatory, a prestigious music school in the capital of China. But, according to one of his tutors, he was turned down for "lacking talent." Coincidentally, the same thing had been said to Walt Disney, who was fired from the advertising agency where he was working because, as his boss wrote, he "lacked imagination." This to the man who went on to found his namesake company, which today is home to everything from the Marvel Universe to *Star Wars*!

When you discover *your* ikigai, you're going to have to:

- Understand there are things that won't work out the first time around.
- Accept rejection with a positive attitude, since not everyone will understand you.
- Find people who will believe in you.
- Take advantage of the opportunities that come along.

This brings us back to Lang Lang's story. After that first disappointment, a music teacher from his school put a score of Mozart on the piano to cheer him up and asked him to play one of the movements from the piece. That simple gesture reignited the young pianist's love for the instrument and helped him get his hope back.

When still age nine, he succeeded at getting into the conservatory on the second try. From then on, he made spectacular progress. He won several international competitions and, at just fourteen, he was a featured soloist at the China National Symphony's inaugural concert, with the president of China in the audience and millions of people listening on the radio.

Seeing Lang Lang's career take off, his father brought him to the United States to polish his skills with a teacher in Philadelphia. His chance of a lifetime would come a few years later, when he was seventeen years old.

At the prestigious Ravinia Festival in Highland Park, Illinois, something amazing happened. The legendary pianist André Watts was scheduled to appear, but he fell ill and had to cancel at the last minute. To the surprise of the audience filing into the auditorium, the presenter suddenly announced that a seventeen-year-old pianist had offered to take the master soloist's place to play Tchaikovsky's Concerto no. 1.

Lang Lang's performance was so wonderful that the next day the *Chicago Tribune* newspaper said he was "fabulous . . . exciting . . . and a phenomenal talent."

A star had been born.

Welcome to the 99 Percent Club

Lang Lang's story is amazing, but maybe you're saying to yourself: *Lang Lang already knew what he wanted to devote his life to when he was only two years old... Isn't that unusual?*

If you don't know what you want to do with your life yet, don't panic: You're part of the 99 percent of young people who don't. Welcome to the ikigai hunters' club!

Although there is no predefined map for life's paths—no forks in the road with clearly labeled signs— once you've found your life goal, you'll never feel lost again. Your ikigai will be your compass.

"*Yeah...,*" maybe you're saying to yourself, "*but what if I still don't know what I want to do in the future?*"

That's why we wrote this book. Stay with us and you'll find out the answer.

2.

Discovering Your Ikigai
Is an Ikigai in Itself

"Accept your feelings.
Know your purpose.
And do what needs to be done."

SHOMA MORITA, PSYCHIATRIST,
FOUNDER OF MORITA PSYCHOTHERAPY

Throughout your life you will reach places where many roads meet, and you'll need to choose which one to take. Sometimes you may be confused by the choices and you might not see the signs for each path, including the one you are on.

You may feel like you're walking through fog.

You won't know where you're going because you're not sure where you are.

Don't worry if you feel this way sometimes. Making choices is part of life, and there are times when you'll find it hard to make a choice, or when you may not be ready to make a decision. Before you choose one path, you may want to explore all or some of the paths you see.

By the time they found out what they wanted to do with their lives, the authors of this book themselves had had all sorts of difficulties, crossed many intersections, and changed their plans a bunch of times before sitting down to write this book.

Here are their stories.

HÉCTOR AND FRANCESC IN THE MAZE

When he was a young boy in the 1980s, Héctor enjoyed reading science fiction novels and dreamed of creating a better future for humanity. He drew things from his imagination in his notebooks. Often, he drew a "smart watch" with a powerful built-in computer. At that time, it was just something he imagined.

On his thirteenth birthday, he got his first video game console. He enjoyed playing *Super Mario World* so much that he decided he wanted to be a video game programmer one day. For many years he chased that dream. With the help of books, he taught himself how to program computers and created several video game prototypes. At eighteen he went to college to study information technology.

By the time he graduated, though, he chose a different path and accepted a research scholarship at CERN (European Organization for Nuclear Research) in Switzerland. After that, he continued to do research in a laboratory in Japan.

After a few years at the lab, though, Héctor realized it wasn't something he wanted to devote the rest of his life to.

At age twenty-five, Héctor returned to his first ikigai, working in the video game industry. He shut himself away over several weekends and created a game with Nintendo characters for up to four players. He went to a job interview in Nintendo's Tokyo offices and showed them his prototype game. Nintendo liked it so much they asked Héctor back for a second interview. Everything seemed to be going well until the final interview. A few days later he got a rejection letter.

Over the following years, he was a programmer, a software engineer, a team leader, and even the head of technology at several start-ups, but all of them went out of business, except for one . . .

Héctor was the first Twitter programmer in Japan. In 2007, he created the first international version of Twitter when this social network was still an unknown start-up. Eventually, Héctor decided to write every day about what he was learning from Japanese culture. At twenty-seven, he published his first book, *A Geek in Japan*. Could writing be his new ikigai? The book sold well, but he wasn't convinced of his writing ability.

He continued writing until he got an illness, which made him very tired. For years he didn't have the energy to do much except to go to work to make a living.

He gave up writing.

Then, one day, a traveler with the mysterious nickname Sherpa turned up in Tokyo and arranged to have dinner with Héctor. Sherpa and Héctor had a great time together and became friends. Each time Sherpa traveled to Tokyo, they met up to go for a walk and eat some Japanese delicacies.

Sherpa was the writer Francesc Miralles.

On a stroll around a Japanese island housing a large colony of cats, Francesc said to Héctor, "You're very good at taking weird information and summarizing everything you learn." It was the first time in his life someone had said anything like that to Héctor. From that moment on, Héctor began to believe that maybe writing could become his ikigai. Sometimes people need someone in their lives to confirm to them that they are on the right path.

On another of their walks, they decided to write a book together called *Ikigai*. To date, they have written five books together, published in fifty-six different languages everywhere, and sold almost two million copies worldwide.

Héctor's life plan is to continue writing more and more without worrying too much about where this path will lead him. He knows that writing is part of his ikigai.

As for Francesc, he grew up wanting to be an astronaut and travel to the moon someday. However, that requires studying engineering, math, and science, which didn't appeal to him. This is why, instead, Francesc started college with a major in psychology. At the last minute, he was admitted to his school's journalism program and decided that was the right path for him.

But after only three months, he realized he wasn't interested in what he was studying and dropped out of college. He got a job in downtown Barcelona at a café that was popular with artists. There, he learned to play the piano.

The next year, Francesc began a degree in English philology, which is the study of the history of language. Three years later, he grew bored with English and switched to German.

Although he loved what he was studying, he decided to take a year off before finishing his degree to work as a volunteer in a refugee camp during the Balkan Wars of the 1990s in southeastern Europe.

After getting his degree, ten years after having started college, Francesc's life kept on changing. He worked as a language teacher, a translator, an editor, and a psychology journalist—the combination of two degrees that he didn't complete—until one day he decided to write his first book.

Often, he had the feeling he didn't know where his life was headed. One day a friend said to him, "Francesc, for you, stability comes from change."

Life Is Not a One-Way Road

By telling you about their lives, the authors want you to realize that it is okay if you are the kind of person who needs to try many things before discovering your ikigai.

Some people are practically born with their life

mission, like Lang Lang and the piano. But most people are going to have to pedal a lot and get lost among some paths until they find the one that is right for them.

And maybe that won't be the right path forever.

Life is not a one-way road. When you do find your ikigai, after a few years you may feel as though you have learned as much as you can or gotten as much enjoyment as you can from it. Then you may want to search for a new ikigai.

You may have several ikigais throughout your life, or sometimes none at all. You may feel you are wandering in the wilderness. There may be a time when you grow tired of pedaling without a direction, get off your bike, and say to yourself, *"I don't have any idea where I'm going,"* or *"I don't even know where I want to go."* What should you do then?

To answer that question, read on to learn about a twentieth-century Austrian physician who devoted his life to something fascinating.

Dr. Frankl Has the Answer

In the 1940s, during World War II, Viktor Frankl, a neurologist and psychiatrist, survived imprisonment in several concentration camps. He said he believed he survived because he had a "why" to live. After living through the Holocaust, he wrote a book, *Man's Search for Meaning*. In it he told about his terrible experiences during the war and introduced logotherapy. Logotherapy is a concept based on the theory that the most important motivation for people is the search for meaning in their life.

When World War II was over, many people sought Frankl's help. They had lost a child, a sibling, or their parents. Some had lost almost their entire family. Frankl's mission was to help these grief-stricken people find something new to be enthusiastic about that would give meaning to their life.

When patients explained to Frankl how horrible their lives were, he challenged them with the question "So, why do you want to continue living?"

After getting over their surprise at this question, almost all of them ended up giving some kind of answer such as:

"I need to see my daughter finish her college degree."

"I'm hoping to learn to play the piano—it's a dream I've had since I was a child."

"I still haven't lost hope of falling in love again."

However, some patients were so lost they couldn't

come up with anything and told him, "I have no idea what I like. I don't think I have a mission in life."

"If you have no mission in life," Frankl answered, "I'll give you one—to find it. From this moment on, your mission will be to discover what your purpose in life is."

Maybe you feel that finding your purpose in life is a tough task. If you don't know where to start, keep reading.

3.

Through What You Don't Like, You Get to What You Do Like

*"It is common sense
to take a method and try it.
If it fails, admit it frankly
and try another.
But above all, try something."*

FRANKLIN D. ROOSEVELT,
PRESIDENT OF THE UNITED STATES (1933–1945)

Everybody, even great geniuses, go through mental blocks sometimes, either because they don't know which path to take, or because the paths they take don't lead them anywhere.

When you keep trying different things until you find something that works, that is what is known in science as "trial and error." You try out different possibilities, one after the other, and each time something doesn't work, you are one step closer to finding the solution.

One famous case of trial and error is that of the inventor Thomas Edison, who, while searching for the filament that would give birth to the light bulb, failed time and again, because the material he used either didn't light up or burned out soon after lighting.

When Edison finally managed to light up the world, after countless attempts, people asked him why he hadn't gotten discouraged after so many failures. The famous inventor answered:

"I have not failed. I've just found 10,000 ways that won't work."

An Exercise for Novelists

Mental blocks are also common in the arts. German author Hermann Hesse, for example, hit a stumbling block after finishing the first part of his novel *Siddhartha*, which would end up being read by millions of people. He was halfway through the book and didn't know how to make the second part continue so it would be as powerful as the first.

Hesse's manuscript ended up in a drawer for a couple of years until, finally having thought out his ideas, the author managed to go back to the book and finish it brilliantly.

This happened a century ago. If Hermann Hesse had been a youth attending a writing workshop today, his teacher might have suggested he answer the following question to break his mental block:

"What is *not* going to happen in this novel?"

And the talented student would start to write a list of things, the more the better, that *will not happen* in the story.

The good thing about this exercise is that you can apply it to your own life. At the end of the day, isn't your life a novel that you are starring in as you go along writing the plot?

Imagine you find yourself lost in a forest where you can no longer see the paths within it. Like Edison, you have tried many things and you don't know how to go on.

Following the writer's exercise, ask yourself:

"What am I *not* going to do with my life?"

Next, write down a lot of options that *won't happen*, because through a process of elimination, *through knowing what you don't like, you'll get to what you do like.*

For example, if Héctor and Francesc were asked this question, this is what they'd say *would not happen* in their lives:

"We *won't* be professional soccer players, because we're not young enough anymore to play competitively."

"We *won't* try to be painters like Edward Hopper or Georgia O'Keeffe, because we were never much good at drawing."

"We *won't* work in a bank, or as stock market brokers, and we won't make a living from betting in casinos, either, because we don't like handling money."

The list can be as long as you want. In fact, it's good to have a lot of NOs, because every time you rule out an option, you're a little closer to knowing *what you do like.*

So, now take a sheet of paper and a pen and start to write.

WHAT AM I NOT GOING TO DO WITH MY LIFE?

1. ....
2. ....
3. ....
4. ....
5. ....
6. ....
7. ....
8. ....
9. ....
10. ....

An Encounter with Yourself

In 2011, an intriguing movie called *Another Earth* was released, which imagines the following situation. A second Earth appears next to our planet, as visible to the naked eye as though it were the moon. An expedition goes to that other planet and discovers not only is that world identical to our own, but the same people live there. In other words, you could travel there and find yourself face-to-face with yourself.

Imagine you could talk to yourself. *What would you say to yourself or ask yourself?*

Take your time to answer that.

If you find it hard imagining yourself in that situation, do this exercise:

1.   *Write yourself a long letter explaining to an imaginary guru some of the things that are worrying you the most; include your doubts and questions.*

2.   *Put the letter in an envelope, write your own address on it, stick a stamp on it, and put it in a mailbox.*

3.   *When it gets to your home, imagine that a faraway friend who needs your advice wrote it, not you. You are the guru, so you will write a new letter to answer all the issues raised in the one you have received.*

4.   *Mail this letter back to yourself.*

5.   *When this second letter arrives at your home, read it carefully and really keep in mind*

everything it says. It is a life lesson from the best guru in the world—yourself.

NOTE: You can also do this revealing exercise by sending yourself an email, but it is more effective to write a letter. The days that pass between it being sent and arriving in your mailbox will give your subconscious precious time to think about the answers.

4.

A Clearing in the Woods

"Two roads diverged in a wood, and I—
I took the one less traveled by,
And that has made all the difference."

ROBERT FROST, POET,
"THE ROAD NOT TAKEN"

At the beginning of this book, your path divided into four directions and you headed down the ikigai track. Now you are starting to know what ikigai is all about, but the woods surrounding you have been getting thicker and thicker . . .

You pedal energetically until you come to a clearing in the woods, from which innumerable paths lead off. The place you are in is like a sun radiating in all directions.

Suddenly, there are so many paths to choose from that your head spins. You are so bewildered by all these choices that you haven't realized there is someone else in the woodland clearing.

It's a girl. She has left her bike on the ground and is looking desperately all around her.

"Where should I go?" she says, fixing her frightened eyes on you. "There are so many options in life that I don't know where to go."

"I don't know what to do with my life, either, if that's any help," you try to reassure her.

The searcher introduces herself. Her name is Naomi and she offers to share her picnic with you by the trunk of an old oak tree.

"I'm scared of choosing a path, an option, and then regretting it in the future, you know?" She goes on telling you, "I don't know what I want to be. I don't know if I want to get married or have kids, either, or even where I want to live . . . Maybe I want to spend a few years traveling and seeing the world . . . or is it better to finish studying so I can work and earn money?"

You shrug your shoulders, not knowing how to answer.

She puts down a sandwich and looks at you for a few seconds with an absent expression on her face. You gaze after a butterfly that is fluttering above a flower.

After a few minutes of silence, Naomi finally asks you:

"If you had a tent, food, and water, would you stay in this clearing forever? It's a really nice place. That way you wouldn't have to make any decisions."

You explain to her that remaining at the crossroads is not possible.

"You're right," she says before taking a bite of her sandwich. "We can always correct our route in the future, if we make a mistake. We're on the road to ikigai, but there are so many paths to choose from . . ."

Having stood up after finishing eating, Naomi looks at the blue sky and, feeling the warmth of the sun on her skin, sighs.

"I suppose our path together ends here," she says a little sadly. "But I get the impression we'll meet again, as if there were an invisible thread joining us, no matter where we might be or what we might be doing. Whenever I feel lost, I'll remember you and know that I'm not alone on this adventure. Neither are you."

Then Naomi chooses one of the innumerable paths leading out of the woods. You take your own path and start pedaling.

Don't Stop for Too Long in the Clearing

These woods with innumerable paths are like our life. Sometimes, just like Naomi, we can feel lost when faced with so many options. Or we can have trouble seeing a path when we are passing through some tangled undergrowth.

The clearing where you met Naomi represents the break you may take in your life before making an important decision.

There are students who, on finishing high school, take a year off to decide what to do with the rest of their lives. In Europe you can see many young North American backpackers with the *Let's Go Europe* guidebook. Although they are moving from one country to another, this is their clearing in the woods. They see things as they go along, like you and Naomi did when contemplating the butterfly and the old oak tree, before the time comes to make decisions that will impact their lives.

Maybe someday you too will take an active break, traveling to faraway countries to find yourself. Perhaps you will want to have an experience as a volunteer, working for people in need or on an environmental project for the good of the planet.

It will be very useful to the world for you to experience your woodland clearing this way.

Or maybe you will need to take a much smaller break on the sofa of your house if you happen to feel as lost as Naomi. You may stop for a while to think, but don't ever let the fear of moving on paralyze you for long.

Don't get hung up on watching TV just for the sake of it, wasting the hours away playing video games, eating junk food. If you veg out, by the time you realize it, others will have moved on along the paths of their lives and you will still be in the woodland clearing wondering what to do.

Don't wait around for inspiration to come to you. You have to go looking for inspiration.

Don't wait for your ikigai to find you; it is your mission to look for your destiny, and to work on it every day once you've discovered it.

THE HAPPINESS FORMULA

Human beings have never had so much information or as many options as they do now. From a cell phone you can access hundreds of millions of web pages, social network profiles, videos, games, entertainment, and more. But does that make us happier?

As with Naomi in the woods, there are so many choices that we get stressed out having to decide among them. In this stream of information, we also feel forced to follow people we don't know, give them "likes," make comments, write posts, or upload videos that in turn get a load of "likes" and capture followers and comments.

Wow, that's stressful! This way of communicating and entertaining ourselves makes our free time more like a job at an office.

Our formula for happiness is:

$$HAPPINESS = REALITY - DESIRES$$

In other words, if you are happy with what you have in life and do not desire anything that you don't possess right now, you will be happier than someone who has a lot more than you but still desires things they don't possess.

For example:

Imagine a girl who loves drawing and has just one drawing set and blank notebook for her art; she'll score highly on happiness. She is grateful for what she has and makes the best of it, without wishing for other things.

At the other extreme, a boy who has hundreds of things but always feels bored will not find happiness by getting more stuff. Soon after getting the latest video game or whatever else might be in style, he will have gotten tired of it and will want his parents to buy him other things.

The difference between the two is that the first one finds happiness in what she already has, while the second looks for happiness in what he doesn't have.

With So Many Paths to Choose From, How Do I Pick What Is Right for *Me?*

Naomi asked herself this question in your meeting in the woodland clearing, and maybe you will ask yourself this question more than once throughout your life. Whenever you feel overwhelmed by options, remember the following things:

- *It is natural to be uncertain.* The world is such a changeable and complicated place that it is normal to have doubts, be confused, and have problems. In fact, having problems is part of life. You would be surprised to know how many successful people also feel uncertainty and anxiety.
- *Don't worry too much about the distant future.* What will your life be like twenty years from now if you choose to study this or that? It is almost impossible to answer that

question. You'd be better off asking yourself about the here and now in your life. Will studying this course make you happy? If the answer is yes, then take that course.

- *Make plans for the next three to five years at the most.* Focus on the near future. What are the most important things in your life right now and what would you like to achieve in the coming years? What things do you need to do every day that will bring you closer to accomplishing that goal?

- *Don't be overwhelmed by doubt.* That would be like pitching your tent in the woodland clearing instead of choosing a path to follow. Comparing different options—for example, when choosing what to study— is normal, but set yourself a time limit for making the decision.

- *Focus on the positive aspects of each option.* Each alternative you may be considering has its good and bad points. But don't focus on the bad points, because then it will be harder for you to make a decision. Negative things are guided by our fears and are usually quite unrealistic. Most of the things that we fear never actually happen. It is much better to make a note of the positive aspects of each option and choose the option that looks best to you.

- *You can take the wrong path as many times as necessary.* One of the reasons people worry when faced with a lot of options is that they tend to exaggerate the consequences of a possible failure. Ask yourself, what is the worst that could happen if you are wrong? The answer is nothing—you can change paths in the future if you realize you made a mistake. In fact, to grow as a person and to learn, you will need to make mistakes and corrections as you go along.

In the following chapter, find out about the advantages of failing from an exceptional teacher—Michael Jordan.

5.

Failing Like a Champion

*"If you fall seven times,
get back up eight times."*

JAPANESE SAYING

Considered the greatest basketball player of all time, Michael Jordan played for the Chicago Bulls and the Washington Wizards for fifteen seasons. He broke over 200 records, many of which are still unbeaten decades after he retired.

For example, during his career there were 563 games in which he scored more than 30 points.

In the 1990s, newspapers and television reported on Jordan's records practically each week, but almost never mentioned the mistakes he had made.

After retiring, when reporters asked Jordan how he had managed to be a champion, he surprised everyone by saying:

"I've missed more than 9,000 shots in my career. I've lost almost 300 games. Twenty-six times, I've been trusted to take the game-winning shot and missed. I've failed over and over and over again in my life. And that is why I succeed."

As well as failing to make so many game-winning shots, Michael Jordan is also known for having been one of the most disciplined players when it came to training. He was tireless. He would get up at five in the morning to start to shoot baskets, even if it was a weekend or his day off.

What Does That Person Do That I Don't?

When you see the news or celebrities' social networks, you may sometimes get the feeling there are people who have instant success. The trouble is, you don't get to see the work and discipline that led to the success.

Whenever you see someone successful, think about all the hard work and effort they have put in. Then ask yourself:

What does that person do that I don't?

Most likely you'll find that they incorporated habits into their life or made sacrifices that got them to where they are.

You might not need to get up at five in the morning, like Kobe Bryant did after retirement, but you can learn things from the biographies of successful people that, when applied to your life, will help you to succeed in your ikigai.

And learning to fail is one of them.

If you want to be a champion, you have to train without being afraid of making mistakes. In fact, *the more times you get something wrong, the more you will learn.* The main reason some people stand out from the crowd is that they have practiced their skill more than others have.

People often feel disappointed when things don't work out as they'd like them to. What differentiates a champion from the rest is that the champion is capable of leaving their disappointment behind and trying again. *Their secret is to keep on practicing.*

Failing and learning from your failure is the best fuel for boosting your ikigai. Each time you get something wrong, make an adjustment so you don't make the same mistake in the future. Then remember that you are one less mistake away from the goal you want to achieve.

Greatest Failures

When you are learning something new, especially at the start, ridding yourself of the fear of getting it wrong will help you take a leap forward.

Here are some suggestions for overcoming your fears:

- If you are learning a new language, practice it with native speakers whenever possible, without feeling embarrassed.
- If you are studying for exams, do exercises and pretend you are taking an exam so you realize what your mistakes are when you still have time to correct them.
- If you have joined a sports team, practice more than anyone else before games and official competitions.

If you are old enough that you've already made a lot of mistakes, make a list of "Greatest Failures," adding what you learned from each one of them.

You're probably used to seeing "Greatest Hits" lists in music and other fields, so it might seem strange for you to put together your mistakes chart, but you will find it very useful.

As the economist, speaker, and writer Álex Rovira says, many people do not recover from sudden success, but everybody learns something from failure. What have you learned from your failures?

```
FAILURE
WHAT IT TAUGHT ME
1.......................................................
2.......................................................
3.......................................................
4.......................................................
5.......................................................
```

Powering Up

A video game character becomes stronger the more fights they have. As they fight, they build up experience and level up.

In a way you, too, are like a video game character, building up experience and expertise. You start at level 1, and the more times you fight—win or lose—the more experience and knowledge you will gain to level up in the art of life.

The difference between video games and real life is that in video games the characters can start each battle over and over again when they lose. We have to live with our losses. So carefully choose the battles you want to get involved in and don't be afraid of things going wrong. Each time you fall, you will get back up with more experience and greater wisdom.

As Sylvester Stallone said in the 2006 film *Rocky Balboa*:

"It ain't about how hard you hit, it's about how hard you can get hit and keep moving forward. How much you can take and keep moving forward. That's how winning is done!"

6.

The Explorer's Kit

*"External objects are
incapable of giving complete happiness
to the human heart."*

HINDU PROVERB

Maybe at some time you have heard the story of Siddhartha Gautama, the Indian prince who became Buddha, one of the most influential spiritual masters in the world.

Born in a palace, surrounded by all kinds of luxuries and delicacies, he had everything a human being could possibly imagine. He never lacked for anything. All that he desired was at his disposal, except for one thing: the freedom to leave the palace.

His parents did not want him to see how imperfect life was beyond the palace's protective walls, so they prevented him from going out to see the world.

When he was old enough, however, he disobeyed and

left the palace to discover life. Outside his luxurious palace, Siddhartha saw things he didn't know existed:

- For the first time, he saw an old person and realized that although he was young, someday he too would grow old.
- He saw a sick person. This made him think that, although he was healthy, it was possible to catch diseases.
- He saw a corpse and learned that, although he was alive then, the time would come when he too would die.

These three encounters didn't frighten Siddhartha. Instead, they led him to decide to devote the rest of his life to finding the causes of human suffering so he could help relieve it.

The future Buddha had found his ikigai.

To find the answers he was looking for, Siddhartha couldn't stay in the palace. He had to venture along paths and become an explorer.

He realized this when he met a wandering man. This man was free to do whatever he wanted whenever he wanted, and this freedom was just what Siddhartha needed to learn life's secrets.

Like the young Prince Siddhartha, many people are

born with all the luxuries of the modern world. They have a roof over their heads, they have cell phones that allow them access to all the information in the world, they can talk to anyone and see people's faces in any place in the world in real time, they buy things online, they play video games with people on the other side of the globe, and on and on . . .

However, despite having all these things, some people may feel empty. They may feel a need to explore life beyond these comforts. They need to give meaning to their life, feel fulfilled, and, through discoveries, help others achieve fulfillment as well.

SIDDHARTHA'S EXPLORING KIT

For any goal you set for yourself in life, you will have to "leave the palace" and become an explorer. To do that, like any adventurer getting ready to journey into unknown territory, you need to be properly equipped.

To find your purpose in life and share it with others, there are six tools you need to carry in your backpack. You'll remember what those things are with this IKIGAI acronym:

Imagination
Kaizen
Inspiration
Gratitude
Audacity
Improvisation

Using Siddhartha Gautama's story as your starting point, look at each one of these tools and how you can apply them to your life.

Imagination

Although he was shut away in a palace during his youth, Siddhartha had a vivid imagination. From his window he looked at what was outside: the snowy mountains on the horizon and the life that existed beyond his world.

Everything that was unknown captured his imagination, and this made him envision a world full of adventures. The power of fantasy cheered him up in his moments of boredom.

This tool, which you were also born with, is key to your mission and can give you courage to explore the world.

Here are some ways you can feed your imagination:

- Read books about places that are very different from where you live, or biographies of people who had incredible adventures.
- Watch documentaries about faraway worlds that you have never visted.
- Attend talks by people who have seen and experienced things you don't know about.
- Visualize what you will do at the moment your adventure begins.
- Make notes about your dreams and your fantasies in a special notebook.

In the words of French author Jules Verne, whose literary fantasies foresaw inventions like the submarine, the helicopter, and—even as early as 1863—the internet, "*Anything one man can imagine, other men can make real.*"

KAIZEN

When the young Siddhartha left the palace, he didn't become Buddha right away. He didn't reach enlightenment until he was thirty-five—an old age at that time. He had to work at his mission every day for years to achieve enlightenment. He improved himself as a person by perfecting his meditating technique, slowly but surely.

Siddhartha, without knowing it, applied what the Japanese call *kaizen*. This is a way of improving something little by little every day. Kaizen was used at the Toyota factory in Japan, where all the workers were encouraged to identify small improvements and suggest practical solutions to streamline the production system.

This is believed to be the secret behind Toyota's success in producing the most reliable automobiles in the world.

Maybe you are wondering what that has to do with your life. Actually, it has a lot to do with it, once you start working to improve yourself. Even if you devote only half an hour a day to learning something or improving your skill at something, you'll improve one percent at that task each day. In a 100 days' time, you will have improved 100 percent!

Imagine the progress you would make:

- You could learn a new language.
- Practice a sport.
- Perfect an art (music, painting, writing, etc.).

- Improve personal skills, like knowing how to listen or being capable of putting yourself in someone else's shoes.

If you practice a little every day, kaizen will enable you to develop superpowers!

Inspiration

At first, Siddhartha didn't like facing death, poverty, and sickness. It broke his heart to see so much human suffering. However, instead of feeling sad, seeing all that pain lit a fuse inside him that inspired him to look for solutions so that people would not suffer.

On his long pilgrimage, at no point did he lose faith or the hope of achieving his goal.

Inspiration is the definitive proof that you have found your ikigai.

If you notice that something in your life makes you especially happy, if you feel useful doing it and time flies while you are doing that task, keep the fires of that inspiration burning. Follow that path and stoke the fire.

On the other hand, if you notice that something bores you or you don't have an interest in it, try to change it or find something that does interest you.

Inspiration is a dream that makes you never lose sight of the port you want to reach. It is a lighthouse on the horizon guiding your life.

GRATITUDE

Siddhartha came across many people who helped him along his way, guiding him and teaching him until he became Buddha. He always thanked them warmly, no matter how much or little they had given him, and even devoted time to meditating while focusing on gratitude. It is said that once, as the day drew to a close, he told to his followers:

"Let us give thanks, because if we didn't learn much today, at least we learned a little, and if we didn't learn a little, at least we didn't get sick, and if we got sick, at least we didn't die—therefore let us give thanks."

The more you thank people, and the happier you make them, the easier it will be for you to see the bright side of life. Gratitude makes us focus on beautiful things, and in that way we find more and more reasons to be grateful.

Héctor and Francesc made a short list of the things they both feel grateful for:

- Having met, which gave them the gift of a friendship at a distance of 6,214 miles (10,000 kilometers) and many shared adventures in the shape of trips or books.
- Having a book translated into fifty-six languages, which means many, many people around the world can read it.
- Knowing that readers support and give life to this book, and that what they are reading in these pages will help them find direction in life.

And you? What are you grateful for in life? Even the smallest thing counts!

AUDACITY

It took a large dose of courage for Siddhartha to swap the comforts of the palace for uncertain paths, but thanks to that he discovered a life philosophy that has enlightened and inspired hundreds of millions of people.

There are many emotions people feel, but by greatly simplifying them, they can be divided into fear (rejection) and love (attraction).

Both fear and love, especially when they are very powerful, sometimes make us do strange things. A strong person is someone who is able to identify when emotions are overwhelming them inside and making them act irrationally.

Maybe the greatest form of being brave is asking yourself tough questions and daring to answer them. Here are some examples:

- Why don't I do what I had aimed to do, knowing how important it is for me?
- Why don't I dare talk to that person I like so much?
- Why do I find it so hard to talk or sing in public?

The answer to all these questions is usually that we are afraid of something, such as making fools of ourselves, failing, or being judged negatively by others.

To fight this fear we can nurture love. A mountaineer overcomes their fear of a high peak thanks to the love they feel for the mountain, which transforms fear into its opposite—bravery.

Brave people dare to do what others fear. They have the power to change themselves and to change the world.

Do you dare to be like them?

Improvisation

Are things not going well? Do you get bored always doing the same thing? Would you like to go beyond the world you know? Do what Siddhartha did and jump in headfirst to discover new paths.

You can change your path as many times as you want. Each time you feel your days have become predictable or that you are no longer learning anything new, improvise!

Do something you have never done before, or do something that you have done, but this time do it in a completely different way. If you take the first step toward the unknown, a new world will open up beneath your feet.

If you are following a path bordered by long grass that you can't see over, improvise! Jump into the brush and find a new path.

Living means creating and destroying paths along the way. A strong explorative mind is able to improvise and move among the changing paths without fear.

To paraphrase a saying that is attributed to the genius Albert Einstein, *if you do the same thing over and over again, don't expect different results.*

7.

The Seventh Tool: Revealing Yourself to the World

*"Do not allow people to dim your shine
because they are blinded.
Tell them to put on some sunglasses."*

LADY GAGA, SINGER, SONGWRITER, ACTRESS

Imagine that the best soccer player or singer in the world lived on a desert island without anyone knowing about their talent. Wouldn't that be a shame?

Well, the same thing happens to people who don't dare to reveal themselves to the world. There are painters who collect paintings in their basement that beauty will forever go unappreciated, writers with several novels written that no one has ever read, photographers whose pictures will never be seen by anyone.

Don't become a person who is afraid of showing the world what you do!

FORGET ABOUT "WHAT THEY WILL SAY"

Often people don't do something because they are worried about what others will say if they show who they really are. A person might think, *"What if I make a fool of myself? What if I don't have what it takes? What if I'm not good enough?"*

All these questions stem from a little voice inside them that they should never listen to, because it serves no purpose. It simply acts as an excuse for not doing stuff.

Do you think Venus and Serena Williams played great in their first match?

And isn't it true that before the moon landing there were lots of dress rehearsals that ended in utter failure?

Everyone who has managed to be successful faced up to the initial fear of exposing themselves to the world when they were still not the best. When we see someone at the top of their game, we are not mindful of their beginnings, when they knew nothing and were rookies. Nor do we see the hours, days, and years of continuous effort that laid the groundwork for their success.

The Invisible Ladder

Imagine Arnold Schwarzenegger doing his first squat in his hometown in Austria or weightlifting for the first time as a teenager. He could hardly do it! But this is an Arnold we have never seen. Maybe we know he was an internationally famous bodybuilder, as well as being proclaimed Mr. Universe when he was twenty years old. We know a lot more about his acting side, from his debut with *Conan the Barbarian* to the Terminator series, before he gave up making movies to be the governor of California.

Similar to how we usually only see people's successes and not their failures on social networks, we only know about Arnold's successes, not the long and laborious ladder that, step by step, brought him fame and fortune.

One of the keys to Arnold Schwarzenegger's success was his starting to reveal himself to the world in competitions at a very young age. He didn't win the first competitions, but they helped him learn as he went along and to gain confidence in himself. He never gave up, trained more than anyone, and over time became the most ripped man in the world.

Later on he decided to reveal himself to the world

even more and immigrated to the United States to begin his career as an actor. At first, he was criticized for poor acting, but over time he developed his own style and became a popular idol for millions. In his own words:

"What we face may seem insurmountable. But I learned that we are always stronger than we know."

JUSTIN BIEBER'S STAR

Another success story involves Justin Bieber. When he was a kid, he didn't know how to sing and had to learn from scratch. He sang out of tune and was embarrassed by others hearing him. Despite this, he learned to play the piano, the drums, the guitar, and the trumpet.

When he turned twelve, he was brave enough to sing in public for the first time in a local competition where he lived in Canada. He didn't win but he finished second. The most important thing about that day was that Justin's mom made a video of her son singing in the competition and uploaded it to YouTube.

The video "broke" the internet, getting millions of

hits. A decade later, Justin had become one of the most acclaimed pop artists in the world.

YOUNG HEROES

Girls and boys around the world, even in the most difficult circumstances, have shown us who they really are, and have shown us the power that individuals have to change the world.

Malala Yousafzai, the Pakistani activist, blogger, and university student who was the victim of a terrorist attack at just fifteen years old, once said:

"If one man can destroy everything, why can't one girl change it? (. . .) One child, one teacher, one book, one pen can change the world."

We have another example of everyday heroes in Greta Thunberg, a teenager who is inspiring the entire world with her visions:

"The moment we decide to fulfil something, we can do anything. And I'm sure the moment we start behaving as if we were in an emergency, we can avoid climate and

ecological catastrophe. Humans are very adaptable: we can still fix this. But the opportunity to do so will not last for long. We must start today. We have no more excuses."

Malala and Greta have not been afraid of revealing themselves to the world. They have not been afraid of showing us what they do. And they do really important work!

If Arnold had stayed in Austria training with his buddies, he wouldn't have been anything more than the village muscleman.

If Justin Bieber had stayed in his bedroom playing the piano alone, if he hadn't gone to a local music competition, if his mom hadn't uploaded a video to YouTube of her son singing, we would never have known about him and his true potential would not have been realized.

If Malala and Greta hadn't become public figures and exposed themselves, the world today would probably be a worse place.

GET IT WRONG!

Don't spend time wondering whether you are "good enough" to show what you do. You don't need to do it perfectly—you are on a learning curve. Get it wrong!

You must be thinking: *"What? Really?"* The answer is yes! You should let yourself do something imperfectly, so that in time you end up becoming an ace at it.

To sum up, if you want to be very good at something, you first have to allow yourself to be bad at it. And even if you don't want to show it in public, you can share it with friends or with someone you might know who is an expert in the matter and can give you pointers so you can do it better.

If you don't feel embarrassed the first time you do something in public, that means you probably took too long to do it.

Paths for Revealing Yourself to the World

In addition to letting yourself "get it wrong" and learning from your mistakes, you should begin showing people what you do in small ways, and then gradually do more and more.

These days it's easier than ever before to show people what you do. You may start with something simple like a blog or YouTube channel. Don't expect to have thousands of followers from the start. Focus on doing your skill the best you can, even if your audience is made up of ten people. There weren't many more people at a lot of pop stars' first gigs!

And don't confine yourself to the digital world. Go out to meet people, take part in contests, go to talks and exhibitions, find out what other people are doing.

Here are some ideas for how to begin:

- *If you want to be a scientist.* Besides studying your chosen subject get into the habit of reading scientific articles, so that when the time comes, you'll be ready to write them.
- *If you want to be a journalist.* Start to publish on your blog and in local magazines or newspapers.
- *If you want to be a YouTuber.* Start your channel and schedule the videos you're going to upload.
- *If you want to be a singer.* Practice at home and get used to participating in local competitions so that you lose your stage fright. Join a local music group.
- *If you want to be a writer.* Start by publishing short texts on social networks. Go to a writing workshop, where you will learn techniques and meet other people who share your interests. Take part in a writing contest.
- *If you want to be a chef.* Prepare some dishes with a parent and have some of your friends over to try them out.

Ignore the Trolls

When you reveal yourself to the world, people will inevitably make comments about what you are doing. Some of the comments might not be flattering, and you may feel hurt at first, but you can learn from negative comments. Also, keep in mind that for one negative comment, you may receive ten positive comments! Simply ignore the negative notes and focus on the positive ones, which will fuel the fire of your ikigai.

THE PRACTICE OF IKIGAI

PART TWO

I.

And Now What?

*"Don't aim for success if you want it;
just do what you love and believe in,
and it will come naturally."*

DAVID FROST, BRITISH TV HOST,
JOURNALIST, WRITER

Once you know what you like, what should you do next?

Maybe, at first, the word *work* doesn't sound great to you. But that is just because we usually associate it with things we don't like. Work is annoying when . . .

- On the weekend you have a stack of homework to do on a subject that you don't like or find hard to understand.
- You have to study the night before an exam, when what you'd like to do is watch a movie or hang out with friends.

What happens, though, when every day you work on the thing you love?

Think of a soccer player who has fun at each practice and goes home tired but happy. Or a painter for whom the hours fly by when they're sitting in front of the canvas, utterly absorbed in their creation.

Is that work? Yes, but it is *not just work*. It is also *passion* and *ikigai,* which magically transform any effort into exciting fun, like being at the best theme park in the world.

Confucius, a great thinker of ancient China, said: *"Choose a job you love, and you will never have to work a day in your life."*

It's a Good Sign if You Flow

Do you remember Naomi in the woodland clearing? She was bewildered by so many paths and didn't know which one to take. That may happen to you when you don't know what you like, but it may also happen when you like lots of things at the same time, which is not a bad thing at all.

How can you tell if a hobby or fun activity may be your ikigai?

There is a test that can help you figure that out. If you feel *flow* with what you are doing, maybe you have found the job—in the good sense of the word—for you. What is flow? It is what you feel when you're working at something you love doing and which might actually be your ikigai. It is a theory by Mihály Csíkszentmihályi, a psychologist and researcher. This is what you feel when you flow:

- *Time flies by.* You start to do something and dinnertime comes around before you know it.
- *You are very focused and nothing distracts you.* Like when you are engrossed in a video game you love, or in the middle of an exciting movie; you don't do anything else during that time.
- *Your task is neither very easy nor very difficult for you.* Things that are too easy are boring. Things that are too complicated make people freeze up. We flow when the thing we are doing poses some kind of a challenge, but we are still able to do it.
- *You hardly get tired.* When you love something and it makes you flow, it doesn't take any effort. If, for example, you're crazy about soccer, you'll feel tired when the game is over, but while you're playing, you won't notice any exhaustion at all.

Choose How Far You Want to Go

If you notice all this when you're doing something, you have already found your passion, your ikigai. Now what? Well, that depends on what you want to do with it. To find that out, ask yourself the following question: *On a scale from 1 to 10, how much do I like this?*

Depending on your answer, you'll see how important it is to you.

- *0 to 4*: IT IS A WHIM. Are you sure you like it, or is it just a brief interest? Since you haven't even given it a 5, maybe it's just an amusement.
- *5 to 7*: IT IS A HOBBY. It is a pastime, something nice to do in your free time. If you spend time without doing it, you don't really feel like you're missing something important.
- *8 to 9*: IT IS A PASSION. Now we're talking about something you REALLY like. It makes you flow. It is important in your life and you need to devote time to it because you enjoy it.
- *10*: IT IS A NECESSITY. You find it hard to think about anything else, at least in your free time. Right now it is your reason for living—your passion. You would be prepared to do anything for it.

If you scored from 8 to 10, you are working on something important. Congratulations to you! Not just for having found something that gives meaning to your life, but also because it will bring you many moments of happiness.

Maybe you like what you are doing so much that you wish it could become your job, which will never seem like "work" to you. To do that, you will need to practice until you become very skilled at it, until you become a master at it.

Read on to discover how to master what you love.

2.
How to Unlock
Your Talent

*"The only place success
comes before work
is in the dictionary."*

VINCE LOMBARDI,
FORMER NFL COACH

*"The big secret in life
is that there is no big secret.
Whatever your goal,
you can get there
if you're willing to work."*

OPRAH WINFREY

You've probably heard of these celebrities:

- *Lady Gaga.* With over 27 million records sold, her gigs are always sold out, and the movie *A Star Is Born,* which she starred in with Bradley Cooper, made $436 million.

- *Simone Biles.* Called the best female gymnast of all time, Simone began competing in elite gymnastics when she was ten years old. Since then, she has won more medals in this sport than any other American, including five medals at the Olympics in 2016 in Rio de Janeiro, Brazil.
- *Elon Musk.* A founder of the Tesla electric automobile manufacturer, among many other companies, his SpaceX is the world's largest private space exploration company. SpaceX aims to put a colony of one million people on Mars.

The list of great people who achieve things that others find impossible could be very long. One thing all these people share is that they have invested thousands of hours in their ikigai—their passion and driving force in life. That has enabled them to be the best at what they do, innovate, and in many cases make a good living.

Each one is a master in their field. But how many hours are needed to be as successful as them?

The 10,000-Hour Rule

The Canadian journalist Malcolm Gladwell devoted himself to studying this question. After doing the math, he came to the conclusion that you need to spend at least 10,000 hours on something to become a master.

In his book *Outliers* he gives the example of two very different people born many years apart—Austrian composer Wolfgang Amadeus Mozart and Microsoft cofounder Bill Gates.

Many people who read this study noted that Mozart, like Lang Lang, was a child prodigy of music. Gladwell replied, yes, he was a genius who started to compose at the age of seven, but he wrote his symphonies, which are considered masterpieces, from the age of twenty-one. At that age he had already been playing and composing for 10,000 hours.

As for Bill Gates, he had the great fortune to have computers at his school, which was something very unusual when he grew up, during the 1960s and '70s.

That enabled him to practice all the hours he could, even during his vacations, which meant that when he got to Harvard University he had been programming for five years.

After enthusiastically achieving his 10,000 hours, he managed to create the world's most successful software company.

GANBARIMASU!

The 10,000-hour rule would not deter the Japanese, who are known for their perseverance. They know that fulfillment in life is not just about dreaming and having projects. You have to keep pursuing your dreams until you make them come true. That explains how, after the devastation of World War II, Japan managed to become the third-largest economy in the world.

In Japan, this quality is called *ganbarimasu*, and most of the manga and anime heroes have it—they fight for their goals without losing heart. Unknowingly, they follow the 10,000-hour rule to gain wisdom and skills until they become the best.

One of the many examples is the Japanese manga and anime series *Naruto*. The teenage ninja wants to become the *Hokage*, the village chief, through patient practice. This follows the Japanese saying, *"If you want to heat a rock, sit on it for 100 years."*

In Japan, when someone is about to go into an exam

or a karate tournament, people say *"Ganbarimasu!"* to them, which means "Do the best you can!"

This encouragement to make an effort is much more useful than the typical phrase "Good luck!" That's because luck is not in your control. It's a matter of chance, such as when the only subject you have studied closely for comes up in an exam.

Working hard and doing the best you can, on the other hand, is in your control. This is the path that heroes choose. Are you ready to be one, living the *ganbarimasu* way?

Your 10,000-Hour Plan to Be a Master

If your answer is yes, first work out how many hours your path to mastery will take. The following example shows you what you'll achieve with each hour you add to your practice log.

Imagine your goal is to learn Japanese. This is what you would achieve:

- *With 1 hour.* You will learn some basic expressions like "Hello," "Good night," "Thanks," or "Please," which are very useful if you visit the country.

- *With 10 hours.* You will be able to maintain a short conversation, since you will know how to introduce yourself, request what you need, and ask some important questions.
- *With 100 hours.* You will reach a basic level of Japanese, which will no longer seem so unfamiliar to you. You will even know the most important written characters, or *kanjis.*
- *With 1,000 hours.* Your command of the language will be strong. You will be able to talk about anything, with anybody, anywhere.
- *With 10,000 hours.* You will be a real master of the subject. You can be a teacher, translate books, or give talks about the Japanese language.

You can apply the same calculation to learning anything you love: soccer, video game programming, dance, and others.

How long does it take to reach 10,000 hours in order to be the Mozart of that thing you like so much?

But it also depends on how many hours you devote to what you want to learn each day. In their book *The Ikigai Journey*, Héctor and Francesc made the following calculations:

- 8 hours a day x 5 days a week = 5 years
- 4 hours a day x 5 days a week = 10 years
- 2 hours a day x 5 days a week = 20 years
- 1 hour a day x 5 days a week = 40 years

If you are going to school, clearly you cannot devote eight hours a day to your ikigai. But if you have a couple of hours a day, before you reach the halfway point in your life, you will already be a master at whatever you may have set out to do.

And best of all, you will have fun along the way. If what you have chosen warms your heart, you will be happy from the very first hour of practice. And isn't that a huge success in itself?

3.

Analog Happiness

*"There's nothing better than live music.
It's raw energy,
and raw energy feeds the soul."*

DHANI JONES,
FORMER NFL LINEBACKER, ENTREPRENEUR

Hans Christian Andersen wrote such unforgettable stories that we still read two centuries later, like "The Little Mermaid." And he wrote one of the most beautiful ones, "The Nightingale," in a single day in 1843.

Apparently, the idea came to him while he was strolling through the Tivoli, an amusement park in the center of Copenhagen, which had opened that very summer. It was designed to look like a Chinese garden, which may have served as the inspiration for the beautiful story's setting.

The lead character in this tale is an emperor of China. He had read in books written by travelers that there was no birdsong more divine than that of a certain nightingale that lived in the emperor's very own garden.

"The books say that the nightingale is the best thing about my empire," he said to his head servant. "Why have I not been told of it?"

So he ordered it to be brought to sing in his royal chambers that very night.

The bird was found and invited to a great party that night at the palace, where a golden perch awaited it on which to give its performance.

The emperor gestured for it to begin. When the nightingale sang, all those present cried with emotion, including the emperor. The birdsong was such a great success that it was decided the bird would stay to live at court and would be entitled to leave its luxurious cage twice during the day and once at night, with twelve servants at its disposal.

This brought the emperor much joy, until one day he received a strange gift—a mechanical nightingale, similar to the live one, but covered in diamonds, rubies, and sapphires. When he wound it, it sang the same tune as the real one, while lifting its tail up and down.

The emperor was so delighted with his new toy that he let the real nightingale leave.

But one day the mechanical nightingale finally broke down, and nobody at court knew how to fix it.

Deprived of its singing, the king became deathly ill to the point where he could no longer get up out of his bed. He was overcome with sadness. Everyone in his kingdom believed the old sovereign would die very soon.

When the nightingale heard this sad news, it flew to visit the emperor, and from his bedroom window once again regaled him with its marvelous singing.

The king felt his heart fill with happiness once more. He slept contentedly, recovered his appetite, and soon got his strength back while the bird continued singing to him from a nearby branch.

Ashamed for having banished it in favor of the mechanical toy, the emperor asked the nightingale to stay with him forever, with the freedom to come and sing whenever it felt like it.

Screens Are Our Cage

Almost 200 years have gone by since Andersen wrote this tale, but its message is still relevant today.

Instead of enjoying life in its natural state, we have

replaced it with the virtual reality that we see on our screens. And the consequences are as follows:

- Instead of walking along the street, looking at the sky, the trees, and the changing seasons, people are glued to their cell phones, sometimes bumping into other people who are equally robot-like.
- Instead of talking to the people we love, looking into each other's eyes, we do it on social networks, where we might have thousands of friends, but none of them can give us a real hug.
- Instead of experiencing the wonders of the world "live," like the emperor in the fairy tale we prefer to see them prerecorded on a smartphone or tablet, blind to everything that is out there.

No doubt, these technological advances have brought us enormous benefits, but if we "get hooked" on them instead of using them as a tool when needed, they become a cage that cuts us off from the rest of the world.

THE DIGITAL DIET

Spending all day playing around with a smartphone or video game console, eyes glued to the screen, numbs our brain and tires us out. Hypnotized by that virtual world, like the mechanical nightingale, we stop making an effort—there is no *ganbarimasu*—and we may lose our drive for life, just like the king in the story.

In order to live your ikigai and become a master of what you are passionate about, you will have to get out into the world to feed yourself with fresh ideas and broaden your horizons.

This doesn't mean you have to give up technology. Just set limits to your use of it, so that technology serves us rather than us serving it.

To achieve that balance, there are increasing numbers of people who are practicing the "digital diet." That means they try to set limits on their screen time so they can start to enjoy life again.

The American speaker and writer Brendon Burchard suggests these ways of limiting your screen time:

- Don't check your email for the first hour after you get up.
- Don't look at a screen for the last 90 minutes before going to bed.

- Walk around for 30 to 45 minutes a day without taking your cell phone with you.
- Do the digital diet several days a month. On each of those days, live as if digital devices didn't exist.
- Don't look at your phone during meals or whenever you are interacting with another human being.

Analog Adventures

Oscar Wilde, another great storyteller of the 19th century, said,

"To live is the rarest thing in the world. Most people exist, that is all."

When you are trapped by machines all day long, on autopilot, maybe you are in this world, but you are missing out on what is best about life, you are not belonging. And artists, inventors, and masters need the inspiration the world gives them to fill themselves with energy and new ideas.

Just as photography can be digital or analog—using a roll of film in a camera that is developed for paper copies—here are some other analog adventures to inspire you:

- *Write in your notebook.* In a journal, write down all your plans. You can also write down your thoughts or even a story to read out loud later to your friends.
- *Go on an excursion with a map.* Go somewhere with a parent or guardian, using a traditional map instead of an app. It can be in the countryside or even in a city. You will feel like the great explorers of unknown territories.
- *Read print books.* When you are traveling somewhere or before going to bed, focus your five senses on reading, with no other stimulus than the tale that is told as you turn the pages. You will see how this kind of reading has a great soothing power.
- *Organize analog events with friends.* It's fine to socialize online, but the true adventures these days are real encounters. Invite your friends to come over for a board game tournament or to meet up in a park. Any excuse will do to celebrate friendship in person.

On your path to ikigai, do a little digital dieting and open the doors to life outside. There is a world of surprises waiting for you!

4.

Welcome,
Little Grasshopper!

*"Fear is the enemy,
trust is the armor."*

MASTER PO (*KUNG FU*)

Those of you with fond memories of the Dragon Ball manga and anime series know Son Goku. He was raised in the mountains by his grandfather and was taught what he would need to survive when his grandfather was no longer around. His grandpa was like a father to him and at the same time a master who trained him with the best of intentions.

Son Goku learned to hunt, fish, and cook, and to collect firewood for winter, but he didn't discover his true potential.

After his grandfather's death, Son Goku left his house in the mountains for the first time to discover the world with his friend Bulma. This was how he met Muten Roshi, the turtle spirit, a martial arts master who was Son Goku's mentor.

After several fights at the Tenkaichi martial arts tournament and training sessions guided by Muten Roshi, Son Goku ends up being better than Muten Roshi, proving what Leonardo da Vinci said:

"It is a poor disciple indeed that does not leave his master behind!"

However, the student's path does not end here. On the contrary, this is the time when they must seek out other mentors who can open up their heart to other possibilities.

MASTERS AND MENTORS

So what is the difference between a master and a mentor?

The master has more knowledge than the student.

But a mentor also has perspective because they have been to the places you want to go.

If you want to be a soccer player, someone who has played in a league will not only teach you techniques and tricks. They will also tell you about the paths and short-cuts they have taken and warn you about the dangers they have faced.

When you discover what you like the most in the world, maybe you will be able to go part of the way alone, but there will come a time when you will need a master and maybe a mentor. The mentor may know the track you are following and may show you some secrets.

The Muten Roshi in your life could be a family member, a friend, or an expert in what you want to do. The following are qualities a mentor should have:

- They know how to ask good questions.
- They listen carefully to the answers.
- They seek to empower you; that is, to give you confidence so that you feel you have the power to do what you want to do.
- They guide you without telling you exactly what you should do.
- They help you find paths you didn't even know existed.

If the person you have found has most of these characteristics, they will probably be a good mentor.

A Great Little Master

There is a great little master of the big screen who has enlightened the path of several generations. He is not less a master than Obi-Wan Kenobi. Can you guess who he is? He is no less a master than Yoda, Luke Skywalker's Jedi mentor. He is a master with a little body but great wisdom.

This is some of the advice he gives Luke Skywalker for the challenges he will face, and which may help you find your path:

- Fear is the path to the Dark Side. Fear leads to anger. Anger leads to hate. Hate leads to suffering.
- Wars don't make you great. Inside you, there are other ways to win.
- Do. Or do not. There is no try. If you face a challenge by "trying to do it," you have already lost you.

What would Yoda say if he saw you right now?

"Read this book till the end and start to apply ikigai to your life..."

If one day you don't feel like doing something you know you should do, visualize Yoda or Muten Roshi, and to motivate yourself, imagine them reminding you of your mission.

5.

Do You Want to Be a Superhero?

"Comic books to me
are fairy tales for grown-ups."

STAN LEE,

CO-CREATOR OF MARVEL COMICS

There may be times when you give yourself such a tough challenge that you'll have difficulty finding a master or mentor who can help you along your journey. Or there may be times when you just haven't found the right guide and you are facing a challenge such as:

- Trying out for a spot on the starting team of a sport.
- Passing an exam in a subject that you're having a really hard time with.
- Becoming friends with a classmate you like a lot.

Who should you turn to when you are feeling frantic and don't even know what you should do?

There are some unexpected masters who can give you strength in moments like these, and they are the superheroes who have given you so many fun-filled evenings. You can learn from them how to be your best self.

Ten Superpowers to Be a Superhero

What are the most important qualities for being a Marvel superhero? Here they come. As you will notice, the best thing is that they are all within your reach. You can develop each of them if you put your mind to it.

1. RESPONSIBILITY

"With great power comes great responsibility," said Uncle Ben to Peter Parker, the Amazing Spider-Man. So, the first quality you should practice is being responsible for your life and for your acts, making sure you realize what the consequences are. That means don't hurt others or yourself.

2. DETERMINATION

Ganbarimasu, which was discussed earlier in this book, is another great superpower that it's worthwhile to practice. Superheroes never give up, however hard the circumstances may be, and however many enemies they encounter. Even if you fail a thousand times, keep on fighting.

3. HONOR

What makes a superhero different from a supervillain is that superheroes have honor, or principles. They are true to their word and always search for ways to do what is right. Honor should be a prerequisite in the adventure you are contemplating.

4. UNITY

There are feats you can't do on your own, like winning a basketball game or doing a group project. In fact, as you grow up, you will realize you need the help of others for all great projects. That is why superheroes know when they should join forces, for example, like the Avengers, and work together.

5. INFORMATION

Brute force doesn't solve many things. Instead, it is important, especially when you are facing a great danger, to study the situation in depth and have all the data you can. Knowledge is a superpower that will give you the advantage in whatever you set your mind on doing.

6. ACCURACY

Not only do you need to have courage and strength, but you must also know where exactly to direct it. For example, in Marvel Comics, wherever the superhero Hawkeye looks, the arrow follows. If you try to carry out your plans any which way, you may end up crashing. Before jumping in, specify what exactly you want to achieve. Aim well and you will hit the target!

7. STRENGTH

Going to the gym to develop your physical strength is a good plan, but to pursue your adventures you will also need spiritual strength, which is the true superpower. Where can you train in that? Unquestionably, in your mind, by putting into practice everything you are learning about ikigai. Controlling your mind is half the battle.

8. FUTURISM

You might be thinking, *"Gee, what a weird superpower!"* Futurism means not settling for what you know and have now. You must prepare yourself for the coming challenges, like Iron Man, who is forever developing new technology.

9. REBELLION

Superheroes do not accept injustice or limits. In their fight to do good, they rebel and stir things up to save the world and themselves. Well-aimed rebelliousness is what makes the world move forward.

10. COURAGE

The tenth superpower, no less important than the previous ones, is vital for any adventure you may be going on. Just as fear can lead to inaction and stop you from pursuing your goals, courage, or facing up to your problems bravely, will bring the best out in you. You will become an everyday superhero!

PART THREE

THE FOUR CIRCLES

I.

What You Love to Do

"What I know is that if you do work that you love,
and the work fulfills you,
the rest will come."

OPRAH WINFREY

Continuing on with your journey, you are still on your bike. You have crossed idyllic landscapes, passing through meadows and by streams, negotiating mountain passes, and going down dizzyingly steep slopes.

One day, you spy a city on the horizon.

Its skyscrapers are a startling change after you have gotten used to being surrounded by nature for so long.

As you get closer to the city, the traffic and the crowds of people frighten you. However, you find the courage to keep pedaling downtown, while asking yourself what has become of Naomi.

Although you feel uneasy, you think a change will do you good, so you push on into this new adventure.

As you are crossing a bridge, you come across a woman dressed in old, out-of-fashion clothes. You think she must be between fifty and sixty years old. She is sitting on a stool, gazing at the river. Her eyes are focused on the scenery, as if she can see nothing else. She holds a paintbrush in her right hand and a palette of colors in her left hand.

You stop to contemplate the beauty of her painting, and after glancing over at the mighty river flowing through the city, you say to her:

"Your painting is more beautiful than the real thing."

Your words break her concentration, but she smiles before answering you:

"Thank you. Isn't that what makes us human?"

"I don't understand . . ."

"Art, our capacity for creating new worlds, is what sets us apart from animals. Dogs can't paint things that are more beautiful than reality."

"Of course—dogs don't have hands," you say to her.

"And if they had hands, could they draw?"

This last question leaves you thinking for a few moments.

"I don't know . . ."

She laughs and, putting down the paintbrush, goes on:

"If you are human and love to do something, you will always try to make it better than reality." She looks thoughtful, then adds, "But it's not enough just to know what you like. You need three more things."

"Which things?" you ask, intrigued.

"You'll find out soon enough on your path. There's no need for me to reveal any spoilers. That's what you call them, right?"

You nod, awed by this woman's calmness. She might be poor, judging by the clothes she's wearing, but she seems very happy. You wonder if that might be the prize for finding the thing you love and devoting yourself to it.

You also wonder what the other three things you need to know are, apart from *the thing you love to do*, but the painter then says:

"I perceive a lot of wisdom inside you for someone so young. Have you already discovered what your passion is?"

"Not yet. I'm on my quest," you answer without getting off the bike.

The woman then opens her bag and takes out what looks like a shiny coin with an inscription reading WHAT YOU LOVE.

"Here, take this medallion. It will help you find, or I should say, create, your passion. It will also help you remember you shouldn't stop searching for the other ingredients of life."

"Thanks."

You stow the medallion in your backpack and, after waving good-bye to the painter, set off again.

WHAT YOU LOVE

A Meteorite Hardly Ever Falls

As you learned in earlier chapters, don't worry if you still don't know what you love to do, and if you have no great expectations, either. Some people think what you love to do, your passion, will come to you one day like a meteorite that will change your life forever.

In most cases, there is no "eureka" moment in which what you love to do is revealed to you.

For example, the idea of falling in love at first sight is a romantic notion that usually appears in books and movies.

However, in real life, falling in love is usually a gradual process, with mountains of happiness and valleys of tension.

The same goes for the discovery of ikigai.

It is not going to turn up one afternoon from out of nowhere, with you suddenly feeling a connection with some higher force that makes you shout: "Now I know what I want to do with the rest of my life!"

There are very few people who discover what they love in such an instantaneous way. The rest of us have to keep on trying different things and taking note of what we like and what we don't like. We have to explore things through trial and error.

COME ONE, COME ALL!

You have already learned how flowing with something is a clear sign that you like it, and that listing things you don't like to do helps you get to your ikigai through a process of elimination.

You might not be sure about the path you want to take, or you might be going through a period in which you like lots of things. No problem! You can have different ikigais throughout your life, and some of them will meet in space and time.

It is okay if you try out a lot of different things or have a collection of things you love doing and work through them little by little to discover which of them could be the center of your life.

Steve Jobs, who was a cofounder of Apple, is said to have been good at nothing, but there were lots of things he loved: computers, engineering, design, calligraphy, Zen, and innovation.

He was good at finding lots of things he loved, but he wasn't a great expert at any one of them. However, over the years, he brought together everything he had learned in a great project—Apple—that would change the history of technology.

IDEAS FOR FINDING OUT THINGS YOU LOVE TO DO

- Analyze the people you most admire. What do they do? Try doing what they do to see if you enjoy it.
- Is there some topic you're so interested in that you can watch dozens of documentaries about it without getting bored? That might be a clear clue about your passion.
- Try something new each weekend. It can be something

you don't usually do or even something you have never done before, such as ice skating, learning a different language, playing tennis, writing a story, etc.

- Is there an activity that you get excited about days before it even takes place? It is most probably something you love to do and you should devote more time to it.

- Close your eyes for a moment and visualize your perfect day. What do you do when you get up in the morning? What do you do with your time during the day? When you finish the exercise, write on a piece of paper—or in your analog notebook—what you have to do and what you must stop doing in order to have your ideal day.

2.

What You Are
Good At

"What I did have, which others perhaps didn't,
was a capacity for sticking at it, which really is the
point,
not the talent at all.
You have to stick at it."

DORIS LESSING, WRITER

After a few days exploring the city, enjoying its parks, the-
aters, and malls, you start to feel lonely. It is a contradictory
feeling because you are surrounded by millions of people.

You even have a room in a hostel where they take in
travelers like you.

By the light of your bedside table reading lamp, you
take the medallion out of your backpack. It shines like
a little sun, but it seems as lonely as you in the city. The
painter spoke to you of three other things you need to
find. Will each one have a medallion of its own?

A caretaker has told you that the Monastery of the Oracle is a day-long bike ride from the hostel.

"And what kind of monastery is that?" you ask him.

"From what I've heard, it is a place where each wanderer finds out which things they are and aren't good at."

You know right away you need to go there to continue your exploration.

The next morning you set off, following the caretaker's directions, and spend a whole day pedaling through a barren, uninhabited landscape.

Not until evening falls do you see a monastery surrounded by colored flags at the top of a hill.

You get off the bike and push it uphill and, after a great effort, you reach the doors of this holy place.

You leave the bike leaning against a wooden post and walk up the steps to an altar where two candles throw light on a stone question mark.

"The oracle must be around here," you think as you kneel down.

Then you say out loud, "I want to know what I excel at, what I do better than the rest."

After a few minutes of waiting for an answer, there is only silence. Tired by the long bike ride, you close your eyes for a moment.

When you open them again, you see a man dressed in black who looks like a magician. He has a shiny bald head and a kind smile and is observing you from the other side of the altar. To your surprise he says:

"That oracle stuff is just a myth—it's never worked. Neither the oracle nor anyone else will ever be able to tell you for sure what you excel at. Only you can discover that, with a modicum of experience and a smidgen of observation."

Then the wizard puts his right hand inside the lapel of his tunic, takes out a large golden coin, and offers it to you. It carries the inscription WHAT YOU ARE GOOD AT.

"Here, take this medallion," he says, holding his hand out to you. "It will help you in your search. But remember that only you will be able to find the answer."

You accept the coin eagerly and stash it in your backpack together with the first one. When they touch, a word is formed at the intersection of the two medallions. So you figure you are on the right track.

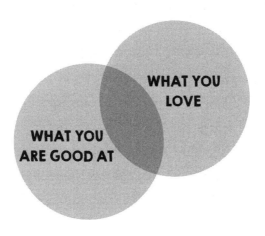

WHAT YOU
LOVE

WHAT YOU
ARE GOOD AT

Before saying farewell, the man who looks like a magician adds:

"If you have gotten this far, it means you still have two medallions to find. I wish you good cheer and strong legs for the path you still have to tread."

Better Than Living on Namek

Imagine you are born on a planet called Namek, which orbits a faraway star. It is inhabited by *Homo sapiens*, but they are special humans with certain genetic modifications.

The moment you are born on Namek, you can walk, speak, and write. From day one, you also know exactly what you are good at and you are hired by a corporation that will employ you for the rest of your life and where you will devote yourself exclusively to what you know how to do well.

Imagine, then, that you have just been born and that right away you sit in front of a computer to program applications that are run by a quantum computer. You are working in a quantum computing company and will do the same thing for the rest of your days, because that is what you do best.

Would you like to be born on Namek? Would you wish for a life like that, where you knew right away what you were good at so you could devote every second of your life to it?

Often we complain because we find learning tough, or even because we don't yet know what we are good at. But it is precisely the act of searching as we go along, the adventure of trying many things in life and discovering different paths, that makes our lives interesting.

If you ever feel down because you don't think you are good at anything, think of the poor old inhabitants of planet Namek, whose destiny is fixed from the moment they are born and whose lives lack emotion. You are lucky!

Know Yourself and You Will Make Progress

Here, on planet Earth, we are lucky to be born knowing pretty much nothing. And that is not a bad thing. There is always something new to learn. The ancient Greek philosopher Socrates said that *the wise man understands that he knows nothing.*

So if you are aware of everything you don't know, then you have made a good start. That doesn't mean you should settle for ignorance.

In the 6th century BCE, at the entrance to the Temple of Apollo in Delphi, Greece, the following maxim was written:

γνωθι σεαυτόν

(gnóthi seautón)

Know thyself

More than 2,500 years later, it is just as valid and useful now as it was then. Because to know what we are good at, we have to start by knowing ourselves.

Now imagine a strange journalist comes to interview

you. He is strange because he asks, "Who are you?" but warns that to answer you cannot use your name, nor the place where you live or were born; nor can you say what your job is or what you study.

How would you answer that question?

"Who are you?"

It is not easy to explain who we are in words, because it is not easy to know ourselves.

The Magic of Feedback

Although knowing yourself is difficult, there is something you can do to learn more about yourself. You can be brave, like a superhero, and *ask others what they think of you*. But don't only ask your friends and family, also ask people who are just acquaintances, so you get other points of view.

If you do this experiment, you must be willing to accept all kinds of opinions, whether they are positive or negative. This information, called feedback, will be useful to you, especially if you ask about something specific that you do.

For example, if you are composing music with your computer, don't hesitate to let others listen to your music. Dare to ask:

- What do you like best about this song?
- What do you like least about it?
- What would you change to improve it?

Listen carefully to other people's opinions and thank them for taking the time to rate your work. Those opinions that point out details you were unaware of will be especially useful.

In the previous chapter you learned how to discover what you love to do. But just because you love doing something doesn't necessarily mean you are very good at it. The world is full of people who aren't good at something they love to do. For example:

- singers who give their all in the shower but who no one would like to listen to in an auditorium
- runners who could never take part in a professional competition
- novelists with more enthusiasm than good ideas
- entrepreneurs with projects that will never make money

You might love doing something because it relaxes you or because you get great fun out of it, but you might not be good at it. In fact, finding something you like to do is relatively easy, compared with being good at it.

The good news is everyone is good at something, although as the wizard at the Monastery of the Oracle says, it is up to each individual to find out what it is. Others' feedback is very useful, but in the end, you are the one who has to look at your face in the mirror to get to know yourself.

Maybe you don't have the physical attributes to ever be a professional basketball player, but you love the sport so much and analyze games so well that you would be an excellent coach.

In fact, as we saw when the first two medallions came together, when you are lucky enough to have *what you love* coincide with *what you are good at*, that becomes a *passion* more than a hobby. We are aware we have a rough diamond in our hands that will dazzle if we polish it.

Knowing yourself is the key to everything. The more you know who you are, the better your contribution to the world, your career, and your life in general will be.

But don't be in a rush. Enjoy the adventure of getting to know yourself and think about how lucky you are compared to the inhabitants of Namek.

3.

What You Can Be Paid For

*"Many people take no care of their money
till they come nearly to the end of it,
and others do just the same with their time."*

JOHANN WOLFGANG VON GOETHE, GERMAN
WRITER AND STATESMAN

After your visit to the Monastery of the Oracle, you continue pedaling through valleys and meadows, passing through forests, serenaded by mysterious birdsong.

You don't see anyone anywhere. It is as though you have entered a forgotten country whose inhabitants are clouds, rocks, and solitary trees contemplating you as you go by.

After crossing an immense plain covered by green grass, you see the first settlement.

The orange-roofed houses splash across the beautiful landscape. They are all small and nondescript, except for a great mansion set apart from the rest. A tower in the center gives it the look of a fortress.

You notice it is surrounded by a garden protected by a high wall.

You are curious to know who lives there. After the exhausting journey, you feel like resting, so you decide to see if anyone is there. The castle is huge; there must be a spare room where you can spend the night.

As soon as you ring the bell, the garden door swings open automatically. You take that to be a good sign.

You cross the garden to the imposing house entrance, behind a golden-barred gate. Next to the door, several luxury automobiles gleam under the midday sun.

A man dressed in a tuxedo comes out to greet you, beaming from ear to ear.

"Welcome to my mansion, dear traveler. Would you like to come in?"

He leads you to an enormous living room, where the sound of your footsteps echoes off the marble walls. The owner of the house invites you to sit down on a sofa next to a window that looks out onto the garden. After serving you a glass of iced tea, he asks you:

"What brings you to these parts?"

"I'm looking for my purpose in life."

"Well, you won't find it here," he says as a sad smile deepens the wrinkles, or lines of experience, on his face. "Maybe instead of seeking your purpose, you should just try to create it."

"Create it . . . but how?" you answer back.

He scowls at you as if he was remembering something unpleasant.

"It is not easy to find your purpose in life. I also tried but failed. I only managed to get one of these medallions."

"Which one?"

Pausing in his explanation, he serves you more tea before getting up. Then he comes back with a box. He opens it on the coffee table for you to see a golden medallion, like yours, with the inscription WHAT YOU CAN BE PAID FOR.

"I'm going to tell you how I got it," he says while he strokes his gray-bearded chin. "When I turned fourteen, I started to read books about investing in the stock exchange. With a loan from my parents, I started to buy and sell shares. After ten years, I managed to get enough money so I did not to have to worry about looking for a job. I could work from home, buying and selling shares from my computer screen. I didn't need to go out. More and more money was getting paid into my bank account.

I bought several houses, each one bigger than the one before, and lots of automobiles. I was making all the money I had dreamed of, and more . . ."

"So why are you sad?" you ask him. "You should be happy."

"I got married and divorced many times without finding true love. I kept on making more and more money, but as time went by I discovered I didn't enjoy my life at all. And now I live shut away in this mansion. I have lots of money in the bank, but no one to share it with." He lets out a long sigh and then adds, "Don't make the same mistake I made. The money medallion is important, but only if you manage to get the other three."

His servants serve you a delicious meal, while the millionaire tells you stories of his life, which are filled with regret and bitterness. He tells you about mistakes he made that he would correct if he could go back in time.

After taking a shower you spend the night in one of the mansion's rooms. The next day you get ready to continue your journey.

The sad millionaire comes out to meet you with the open box.

"Here. I'm giving you my money medallion," he says, showing you the large golden coin gleaming in the dawn light. "It will help you make a living from your job, but that won't make you happy if you don't find the rest of the medallions."

After thanking him warmly, and before getting back on your bike, you put your third medallion with the other two. And you realize that something happens. When WHAT YOU ARE GOOD AT comes together with WHAT YOU CAN BE PAID FOR, the intersection creates a new word.

Making a Living from Your Passion

Perhaps you have heard of Tony Hawk, if you follow skateboarding. However, even if you haven't heard of him, his story is fascinating.

As a kid, Tony was brimming with so much energy that he was always getting into trouble at school. His teachers brought this to his parents' attention, and after a psychological evaluation, he was diagnosed as "hyperactive."

Tony was given various treatments to try to calm him, but nothing worked until one day when his older brother gave him a skateboard.

At just eight years old, Tony began to spend hours and hours practicing every day with the skateboard, and this appeared to solve his hyperactivity problem.

At twelve, he began to compete with his skateboard. At fourteen, he turned pro and was winning prize money and earning money from sponsorship deals. By the time he turned fifteen, he was earning more money than his parents and teachers.

At seventeen, Tony bought his first house with the money he had earned simply by using his skateboard.

In 1999, he was the first person in history to complete

a 900, which is two and a half midair revolutions on the skateboard. That same year, the first video game named after him came out on the market: *Tony Hawk's Pro Skater.*

Tony is over fifty years old today and has made a living from his passion. He has made it his *profession.* But Tony was not only the best in the world at what he did, he was also smart when it came to creating video games, documentaries, a skateboard brand, sports clothing, etc.

Right now he is semiretired and only skateboards for pleasure, making a living thanks to the money his businesses generate. He looks after his money and knows how important that is to do in order to live a carefree life.

For the people who know what they love, are good at it, and manage to get paid for it, this skateboarding genius has the following advice:

- *Lesson 1.* Investing and saving from an early age pays off later on.
- *Lesson 2.* Even if you earn a lot of money, you shouldn't be overconfident. Think about different ways of making money.
- *Lesson 3.* Remember that money is also there to help others (this will be discussed in the next chapter).

Ideas for Starting to Make Money

Even though you are very young, your relationship with money is going to impact your life from now on. Following the example of geniuses like Tony Hawk, here are some recommendations for you on how to manage your money:

- *Start saving early.* Even if you can't buy a house like Tony Hawk did, you can start saving a little every week, and at the end of the year you will have a nice sum in the bank.
- *Start a YouTube channel, a podcast, or a blog. Ask an adult to help you activate the advertising.* At first, you will earn little more than a few dollars a month, but if you start to build up an audience, you will earn more. When you have grown more, you may want to think about looking for brands to sponsor you, or working with other channels, etc.
- *Offer to work for free for people or companies you admire.* It might seem like a contradiction to you, when we are talking about earning money, but many great professionals started out as unpaid students to professionals, or interns. This let them gain experience and

connected them to the industry they were interested in. As your knowledge increases, you will be able to ask for money.

- As you saw with the medallions that you put together thanks to the millionaire, when you are good at something, it becomes your profession once you start to get paid for it.

But does the search for your ikigai and fulfillment end once you find something you like, do it well, and get paid for it until the day you retire?

No, it doesn't. Read on to see what else awaits you. It is anything but unimportant.

4.

What the World Needs

*"I have two hands:
one for me,
one for other people."*

MILLIE BOBBY BROWN, ACTOR AND PRODUCER

You have come to a small seaside town and sit down on a bench facing the beach. It is midafternoon and the people are coming for a walk after work. Watching them walking back and forth, you wonder what each one of these people does for a living.

You can't help thinking about your own future. What will become of you? What kind of life do you want to have?

A man emerges from among the casually dressed strollers and approaches you; he is wearing a hat and a leather jacket and looks like an adventurer. He looks at you with a knowing smile, as if you were childhood buddies.

You look away but then he says to you:

"I know what you're looking for."

Then he asks if he can sit next to you on the bench. You agree, curious about what this guy wants to tell you.

With his eyes fixed on the sea, the man starts to speak:

"I spent years traveling and searching for my ikigai all over the world, until I discovered that what I craved so much had been within touching distance all the time."

"You spent years traveling?" you reply. "You must have seen a lot of countries, then."

The man adjusts his hat and smiles with a melancholy gesture.

"I've been in over a hundred countries and I've contemplated the wonders humanity has created. The disasters, too. I've seen wealth and extreme poverty. I've seen terror, disease, and greed, but also generosity and a lot of happiness. I had to see all of that in order to find myself . . ."

He pauses to breathe in the sea air and continues:

"I learned Japanese at a very young age because the country's culture fascinated me, although I didn't visit it until a short while ago. On my trip I stayed for several days at a temple in Akita. One night, I couldn't sleep because of the sound of the wind blowing against the wooden walls. Wide awake, I went to the main hall of the temple and there, under the light of an oil lamp, was a monk sitting on the tatami mat. Since he couldn't sleep, either, he told me a story which, after I understood it, changed my life forever."

"What story?" you ask eagerly.

"He told me that, a long time ago, one of his ancestors called Mizu lived in that very temple. As a teenager, he trained so he would be accepted as a monk. With him lived another nine pupils who, after years together, were practically like a family. One of the tests they had to go through consisted of climbing to the summit of Mount Fuji to take firewood there."

In your mind you visualize the highest mountain in Japan, with its eternally snowcapped summit. It seems like too tough a test to climb all 12,389 feet (3,776 meters) carrying a weight on your back.

"Apparently, Mizu was tall and well built," the man goes on. "When the day of the test arrived, in the midst of winter, with a meter of snow covering the mountain slopes, Mizu shouldered his part of the firewood and right away took the lead, leaving his nine companions behind. In midafternoon, he reached the summit before anyone else. Overjoyed at knowing he was the winner of the test, the weariness briefly drained out of his body. But there was his master, in a cabin on the edge of the Fuji crater, waiting for him with an angry look on his face."

"Why was he angry?" you ask. "If he had taken the firewood to the summit . . ."

"The monk explained it to him like this: 'You have left your companions behind. Go back down and find them and help them.' To which Mizu replied, 'I have won, and instead of rewarding me, I am punished with having to go back down? It's not fair!' The master took a step forward, covering his eyes with one hand to protect himself from the blizzard, and with the other pointed down at the tiny dots in the snow—the other disciples who still had half the mountain to climb. Then he said, 'You have won nothing, Mizu. Perhaps you are even going to lose everything because of your ineptitude! Look at your friends down there. If night falls and they don't manage to get here, they will freeze to death.'"

"Wow . . . and did he manage to help all his friends?" you ask, intrigued.

"Mizu went back down and helped the others carry the firewood up to the summit. In his diary, he wrote,

'I felt much happier when we all managed to reach the cabin at the summit of Fuji than when I reached it first, believing myself to be the winner.'"

The man becomes emotional recalling the story. You thank him for sharing it with you and then he says to you:

"Before going off and continuing your search, let me give you this medallion that the temple monk gave me after telling me the story of Mizu."

Bursting with emotion, you hold in your hands the last great coin you were missing, with the inscription WHAT THE WORLD NEEDS.

"Remember to take others into account in your plans. A success shared tastes twice as sweet. What the world needs is your help, however little it may be. Whatever you end up doing, that will add meaning to your life and to that of others."

After hugging him gratefully, you run to the nearest post office. All of a sudden, you want to send postcards to your parents and friends.

While you are waiting in line, you take the four medallions out of your backpack and look at them. You notice the intersection of the two last coins has created a new word.

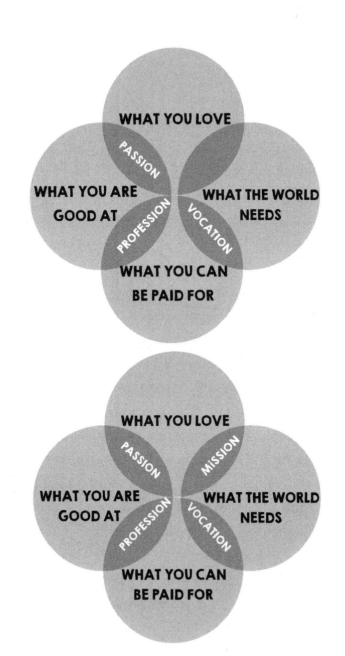

At the same time, the intersection of the fourth medallion with the first also makes another word.

And the magic doesn't stop there, because you realize the four medallions form a flower. And in the middle of the flower a word starts to form . . . However, before you can read it, it's your turn at the post office counter and you hurriedly put the coins away.

Helping Charges Your Batteries

Helping other people is not something only missionaries and volunteers do. And it's not necessary for there to be a great catastrophe before we lend a helping hand. In fact, every day there are chances to make other people happy. Especially those who are closest to you!

And helping other people makes you feel better, too.

When you feel lost in life, helping will make you feel useful and valuable, even if you are just listening carefully to someone who needs to talk.

You've probably experienced what it feels like to make someone else happy. For example, when you get a gift right and see the happiness in the other person's eyes; or when you help someone who couldn't have done something without you. Suddenly, you feel powerful, at peace with yourself, like Mizu after helping his companions climb Mount Fuji.

As the English poet John Donne wrote four centuries ago, "*No man is an island.*" We all need someone's help. That is why the WHAT THE WORLD NEEDS medallion is so important.

DROPS OF HAPPINESS

When we watch the news, the world's problems may seem so big and so numerous that we feel incapable of helping.

The missionary Mother Teresa of Calcutta had an opposite point of view. She said, "*We ourselves feel that what we are doing is just a drop in the ocean. But the ocean would be less because of that missing drop.*"

We tend to underestimate the power that a small act of kindness has to change the world. Let's take a look at a few "drops of happiness" we all can bring to the world:

- We can cheer up a friend or relative who is sad.
- We can listen to someone who needs to talk about a problem.

- We can help someone who has too much work (for example, your parents with the household chores).
- We can stop using packaging or plastics that contaminate the oceans.
- We can take care of trees and animals, our companions on this planet.

Each one of us who hands out these drops of happiness can inspire others with our example, and a lot of drops end up forming a great ocean of love.

Don't try to save the entire world from the start. Begin with little things, such as helping your relatives and friends. Over time, as you develop your ikigai, your sphere of influence will begin to expand and you can be useful to more and more people.

Help the world with your daily actions. The way you act affects your life and other people's lives.

You may have heard of the butterfly effect, which says that the fluttering of a butterfly's wings can cause a hurricane on the other side of the world. This means that each one of your little actions has the potential to expand and spread across distances to change or affect other people.

VOCATION AND MISSION

You saw how when the medallions joined, two new concepts appeared at the intersections. Joining WHAT YOU CAN BE PAID FOR with WHAT THE WORLD NEEDS produces VOCATION.

A vocation is a job that a person feels a strong need to do, like a calling, which often involves helping other people. A vocation can be very fulfilling, and people who have them are often very happy with their work. Following is a list of some professions that are considered vocations:

- *Doctors and nurses.* The act of helping others is seen clearly with healthcare workers. Apart from their efforts to cure patients, the caring treatment doctors and nurses provide to sick and injured people is important and appreciated.
- *Psychologists and therapists.* Your body might be healthy, but you might be suffering emotionally or psychologically, and these professionals can help you with your problems.
- *Teachers.* Many people have found the right career

because a teacher believed in their ability or talent and encouraged them to follow a certain path.

- *Environmental engineers.* In the face of the ecological challenges threatening the planet, such as global warming and pollution, these professionals are vital for saving the earth.
- *Environmental and peace volunteers.* These are people who work in very poor regions of the world or in conflict zones, or fight to save the planet.

When WHAT THE WORLD NEEDS is also WHAT YOU LOVE, then you are lucky because you have a MISSION in life. There is no greater success than that.

Now that you have the four medallions, the journey is almost at an end. But first, there is one more thing to learn.

5.

Connecting the Four Circles

"Life isn't about finding yourself.
Life is about creating yourself."

GEORGE BERNARD SHAW, IRISH PLAYWRIGHT

During the last part of your journey, you were at the post office, sending postcards to friends and relatives to give them a nice surprise. And since then you have seen the concepts that appear every time two of your medallions join.

When you go out into the street and look at the flower that the four medallions form, you see a word appearing. Of course, it is *ikigai.*

You are so hypnotized by this word that you haven't noticed someone seated on a stopped bicycle watching you.

You put the coins back in your backpack, and when you look up, you see her.

WHAT YOU LOVE

PASSION

MISSION

WHAT YOU ARE GOOD AT

IKIGAI

WHAT THE WORLD NEEDS

PROFESSION

VOCATION

WHAT YOU CAN BE PAID FOR

"Naomi!"

"I'm really glad to see you!" she says.

"Me too," you reply. "Did you manage to complete the four ikigai circles?"

Naomi nods proudly. Then you both get on your bikes and head for the train station. The journey has taken you a long way and now it is about time you returned home.

"I'll pay for your ticket," Naomi offers. "I've made some money cutting the grass in yards."

An hour later, after securing the bikes on the train,

you are sitting facing each other next to the window, enjoying the view and sharing the journey taking you back home, each of you heading to your own station.

It is time to discuss your adventure, to share all the things you have learned while you were finding the medallions. Naomi talks without taking her eyes off the scenery rushing past the window.

"We have the theory but now we're missing the practice! Once you discover what your ikigai is, when you know what you want to devote yourself to and you know what your purpose in life is, your passion, vocation, and mission . . . while you are trying to achieve it, what do you do with your life?"

After thinking about it for a few seconds, you reply:

"Maybe it's about bringing ikigai into our day-to-day life, to whatever we do."

"That's right . . ." Naomi answers, then bites her lip. "To live the ikigai way, we will need to learn from true masters."

"Which masters are you talking about?" you ask.

"People who have experienced a lot and lived well, those who always have a *reason* to live and are always in high spirits."

While listening to her, you wonder if people like that exist. You have heard so many complaints over time and so many negative opinions that you find it hard to believe you can lead a long life without losing your enthusiasm and cheerfulness.

"Apparently, they are people who live slowly so they get further," she says, "and who, in the same way they lovingly cultivate their garden, nurture their relationships."

As the train brings you closer to home, you realize the lessons you have learned on your travels will help you find these long-lived masters. Now find out how to apply the teachings of ikigai to your daily life.

PART FOUR

Living the Ikigai Way

I.

The Secrets of the Happy

"Perseverance is strength."

JAPANESE PROVERB

The adventure that led the authors to write this book began in 2015, when they were strolling through a park in Tokyo and chatting about the "village of the centenarians."

A relative had told them about a village of 3,000 inhabitants in the north of Okinawa. This peaceful place, bordered by seashore and forest and inhabited by farmers growing citrus fruits, would not have grabbed the authors' attention if it hadn't been in the book *Guinness World Records*. And it was in the book for a very lovely reason.

Ogimi is the world's number one village when it comes to long life, or longevity. People here have a greater chance of living to one hundred years of age or more than in any other part of the world. That is why it is known as the village of the centenarians.

"What if we went there to interview them to find out why they live so long?" Héctor and Francesc both wondered.

But they didn't just want to speak to the oldest residents. They wanted to see where and how they lived, what they ate, how they interacted with one another.

Several months later, Héctor and Francesc were flying from Tokyo to Naha, the capital of Okinawa, to begin their research. They hired a car to go north, where they would spend as much time as necessary to do the fieldwork.

Since there were no hotels or rooms to rent in Ogimi, they stayed at the House of the Orchids, a beautiful rural property about 7 miles (11.2 kilometers) from the village. At the end of each day in the village, when they returned to the house, the owner's cat was waiting for them and seemed to listen carefully to their conversations about what they had discovered.

Why Do the People of Ogimi Live So Long and So Well?

After finishing their fieldwork and returning home, Héctor and Francesc wrote their book *Ikigai*, which explores why the people of this village are masters of long life. *Ikigai* has been translated into fifty-six languages everywhere. Here is a summary of why these people live so long, based on the authors' conclusions:

- *They live stress-free.* In Ogimi, they don't even have cell phone reception. You have to go up the hill where the weather station is if you want to read WhatsApp messages.
- *They spend a lot of time outdoors.* They take care of their gardens, walk to their neighbors' houses, work in the fields, etc., breathing fresh air all day long.
- *They exercise.* Early in the morning, they follow exercise routines from *Radio Taisho*, a regional television program named for a show that used to be heard on the radio.
- *They stop eating when they are 80 percent of the way to being full.* *Hara hachi bu*, as it is known, consists of

not eating too much. The villagers don't go hungry, but they save a little of their appetite for the next meal. This keeps them livelier and lighter on their feet.

- *They nurture friendships.* Not an afternoon goes by without friends getting together to play gateball, a game like croquet, or to sing karaoke or celebrate a birthday. Ogimi's inhabitants never feel lonely.

- *They don't retire.* As they get older, they work less, but they never stop doing the things they like.

- *They follow their ikigai.* They know their passions. Since Ogimi is a rural place, for many people their passion is their vegetable gardens. Their friends are also part of their ikigai, and every day people spend time with each other. They look forward to what they do each day, so they are eager to get up in the morning.

Seven Rules to Happily Live for a Hundred Years

The place where you live is probably very different from this little farmers' village, but there are things you can do to live like these Japanese centenarians. Here are some of their secrets to include in your daily life:

1. SWITCH YOUR CELL PHONE OFF ONCE IN A WHILE.

2. GET CLOSE TO NATURE AS OFTEN AS YOU CAN.

3. PRACTICE A LITTLE EXERCISE REGULARLY.

4. AVOID OVEREATING (ESPECIALLY JUNK FOOD).

5. MAKE GOOD FRIENDS.

6. DON'T STOP DOING WHAT YOU LIKE.

7. LIVE YOUR IKIGAI.

2.

Don't Rush Toward Your Ikigai

"It does not matter how slowly you go,
so long as you do not stop."

CONFUCIUS, CHINESE PHILOSOPHER

There are people who mistakenly believe that being active means always running around. When it comes to your ikigai, once you discover your life goal, the last thing you should do is hurry.

If you rush, you will miss many details that may be important to your goal.

In her book *Time Mindfulness*, Cristina Benito quotes a fable that illustrates this problem very well:

> *An explorer, who was anxious to get to the*
> *heart of Africa as soon as possible, offered the*
> *expedition porters a bonus so they would walk*
> *more quickly. They obeyed him for several*

*days, but one evening they sat down on the
ground and refused to continue.*

*When the explorer asked them to explain
themselves, they answered:
"We have walked so quickly we no longer
know what we are doing. Now we have to
wait for our souls to catch up."*

That is exactly what happens when we are in a mad
rush, doing a thousand things at once with our head
elsewhere. We no longer know what we are doing, and
perhaps, like the porters, we have forgotten the reason
we are going somewhere to begin with.

THE CREATOR OF GAME BOY

The opposite of hyperactivity, which makes us run around
like headless chickens, is not laziness but *active slowness*.
That is, moving little by little, as Confucius recommends,
but neither stopping nor missing out on anything.

A wonderful example of this is Gunpei Yokoi, who was a
great Nintendo video game designer. He studied electronics

at Doshisha University. After graduating, he began working at Nintendo in 1965 on the Hanafuda playing cards assembly line. At that time, Nintendo made cards.

Gunpei was an incredibly patient man, as well as observant. He practiced active slowness and didn't waste his time. In addition to supervising the assembly line, he also created a toy for his own amusement. It was an extending arm.

One day, when the Nintendo chairman was visiting the factory, Gunpei's toy grabbed his attention and he decided to produce it and sell it at Christmas. The extending arm was a great success, and Gunpei became a key designer of new toys.

When he was at the company as well as when he was away from it, Gunpei remained patient and maintained his powers of observation. It was this slow-living method that enabled him to notice a certain passenger when he was traveling on a train.

He noticed an office clerk typing on a calculator. It was nothing out of the ordinary, but it gave Gunpei a great idea.

While watching the clerk, it occurred to Gunpei that calculator technology could be used to create a toy video game.

When he got back to the Nintendo offices, he worked on creating the first handheld video game console, called Game & Watch, with *Mario* and *Donkey Kong*.

Years later, Gunpei Yokoi created the Game Boy.

ADVANTAGES OF SLOWNESS

The American poet and philosopher Ralph Waldo Emerson said, *"Many eyes go through the meadow, but few see the flowers in it."*

This is why it is so important not to rush toward your ikigai: It is just as important to enjoy yourself along the way as it is to reach the finish line. Maybe what you are really looking for is in a train full of people, as happened with Gunpei Yokoi, rather than at the place at the end of the train ride.

Slowly but surely, as the folk wisdom says.

Practice active slowness and open your eyes. What you are looking for may be much closer than you think.

3.

How to Make Good Friends

"I would rather walk with a friend in the dark, than alone in the light."

HELEN KELLER , AUTHOR AND EDUCATOR

"Friends are those rare people who ask how we are and then wait to hear the answer."

ED CUNNINGHAM, FOOTBALL ANALYST

Friendships are a fundamental part of life and important for ikigai seekers. The ease with which you do your projects will depend on the quality of the people around you.

Ultimately, few things in life are done alone. If you form a band, organize a trip or an outing, or set up your own business someday, you are going to need companions for your adventure.

If you choose them well, things will go as planned and you'll be able to solve any problems together. But if you are surrounded by people who have a negative view of things and with whom you disagree a lot, you won't get much done.

So, do you need to hold a friend audition?

That's going too far, but it is important for you to be aware of the kind of people you have around you. Other people are our mirror, so for example, if you have friends who treat you well and are fun to be around, it's likely they see you the same way.

Tell Me How They Listen to You and I'll Tell You What They Are Like

Something that really defines a person is the way they pay attention to the important things you tell them. We all have dreams and secrets that we reveal to very few people, so their feedback is vital to us.

Imagine you tell a friend about a huge problem. Depending on what your friend is like, you will get one kind of attention or another. Here are examples of different types of people you might encounter:

1. *The one who is miles away.* They pretend they are listening to you, but right away you notice they are not interested in what you are telling them. They are thinking about their own stuff or preparing what they want to tell you when you stop talking.

2. *The wall of silence.* They appear to listen attentively, but then don't give any feedback. They just look at you and, at most, give you a pat on the shoulder and say, "Take it easy, you'll get over it." For some people it's enough to be listened to like this, but other people need more interaction.

3. *The gossip.* They ask a lot of questions, especially about the juiciest details, because it can be great material to tell others. They are more interested in this fun than in what you are telling them. You have to be careful with this kind of listener because they can hurt you.

4. THE DOOMSAYER. This is one of the most dangerous types of people to have around because they only see the negative side of everything. If you talk to them about an exciting project, they will try to stop you from pursuing it by saying things such as:

a) "This is really difficult" or "It can't work." (In reality, what they are telling you is that you are not capable of achieving your goal.)

b) "Are you really sure about what you're doing?" (What they mean is that they think you're going to lose your way and you can't see that.)

c) "Think carefully about it before you take the plunge." (What they really want to tell you is that when you come to your senses, you'll realize this project isn't for you.)

5. THE ANALYST. They help you think. They will listen carefully to you and then start to ask you useful questions to dig more deeply into what you have told them. This will enable you to look at aspects of your life you haven't thought about and help you correct many mistakes. Don't let this kind of vital contributor get away.

6. THE EMPOWERER. This is definitely the champion of friends, and you'll learn more about this type of person in the following section. As the name suggests, when you are in their presence, you feel more powerful because this kind of person makes you believe everything is possible. They make you believe that you can achieve whatever you set your mind to.

How to Recognize an Empowerer

Finding people who follow their ikigai will help you live yours. That is why it is important for you to get together with people who have the same interests as you, and who encourage your dreams or maybe even share them.

Even when someone's plans have nothing to do with yours, you will recognize one of these rare motivational superheroes, the empowerers:

- They listen with real interest and ask questions to understand what you are telling them. The most useful empowerers are the ones who are also analytical.
- They don't make judgment calls or predictions, unless they are positive ones. "I know you can do it" or "You're going to manage it."
- They are truly happy to see you taking risks ("I'm really happy to see you so determined!") and offer you their support from the start.
- If they can, they start to lend you a hand with the crazy idea you've gotten yourself into.

With that said, since we attract people who are like us, the best way to have good friends is to be one yourself. If you are generous, really listen with interest, and try to get the best for your friends, you will create a circle of people around you with those very same qualities.

4.

Experiencing the Love of Your Life

*"We are so different in everything
that we run the risk of falling in love."*

FEDERICO MOCCIA, ITALIAN WRITER,
SCREENWRITER, DIRECTOR

We don't know if at this point in your life you already know what love is or if you have only imagined it. Whatever stage you might be at, we have some bad news for you—sooner or later, *your heart will be broken.*

At the same time, this is good news because you will rarely learn as much about yourself as when you have a romantic failure. If trial and error can be useful to you in your search for ikigai, it is even more useful for finding true love.

You have to meet many types of people before you finally discover the one who is right for you.

Two Pieces of Advice for a Broken Heart

The 2014 movie *Boyhood* is unique and contains an important lesson about love. It was filmed using the same actors over twelve years. That means the child who plays the starring role, Mason, is six years old at the beginning of the movie, and by the end of it he has already turned eighteen.

You literally see life unfold before your eyes.

When Mason grows up and is about to start college, his heart is broken for the first time. His first girlfriend, whom he is deeply in love with, leaves him for an older boy.

Devastated, he tells his dad what has happened, and he gets two pieces of advice:

1. Every minute you devote to crying over a stupid boy or girl is a minute wasted.

2. Do something worthwhile and boys or girls will be lining up at your door.

Ikigai for the Lovesick

The second piece of advice is really important whatever your age, because many people spend their lives looking for someone to "complete" them. That is a big mistake!

If you feel like something is missing, and you lean on someone, when this someone goes away, you will fall over. A person should be complete and self-sufficient so that they are equal to the person they love and can share their path in life.

A quote attributed to the French writer Albert Camus explained it beautifully:

"Don't walk in front of me . . . I may not follow
Don't walk behind me . . . I may not lead

Walk beside me . . . just be my friend"

So when Mason's dad recommends that he does "something worthwhile," he means that Mason should achieve something that makes him feel proud.

If you manage to do something relevant, you won't need the boy or girl of the day to boost your self-esteem. You will be aware of your own worth and you will also be attractive to others without working hard at it.

If you live the ikigai life, love will also be easier for you, because you will have started by loving yourself.

5.
A Time Capsule

*"The future is not
what is going to happen.
but what we are going to do."*

JORGE LUIS BORGES, ARGENTINE WRITER

A few years ago, Héctor and Francesc met life coach Mario Reyes, who used a strange exercise to help his clients work on their life project.

Mario suggested his clients write a letter to their future selves, imagining that fifty years had passed. In the letters, the people would review what had become of their lives by writing a little biography highlighting all their achievements.

By deciding how you want to be remembered, you will know which life you want to lead and which actions you must take for it to happen.

Using this exercise as inspiration, write the following text on a sheet of paper and fill in the gaps about yourself. You can alter it as many times as you need to. Once you have completed it, put it someplace you can see it. For example, on the wall opposite your desk.

MESSAGE TO MYSELF
50 YEARS FROM NOW

Dear . . . . ,

This message has taken so long to reach you because you needed a good chunk of your life to carry out everything you intended to do.

Today you can look back and realize you did it. Congratulations! I never doubted you would make it.

You have managed to. . . . . just as you intended. Of the things you feel the proudest about having done, we can. . . . . and also. . . . .

Although your greatest achievement has definitely been. . . . .

Your work has been very important for. . . . . .and for other people who have followed your example.

For all those reasons, I thank you for everything you have contributed to the world. You have made it a much better place.

With all my love,

. . . .

Epilogue:
Everything Is Still to Be Done

"Plan your future, because that is where you are going to spend the rest of your life."

MARK TWAIN, WRITER, HUMORIST, AND ENTREPRENEUR

You have reached your journey's end. Well, the end of *this* journey, since once you have said good-bye to Naomi and this book, a new adventure begins. The adventure of living your way, following your purpose, and feeding your passion to carry out the mission that will give meaning to your life.

Naomi hugs you before you get off the train. She is moved because she also knows that now begins the most exciting part of your journey.

A very optimistic village elder once told Héctor and Francesc that *everything is still to be done.*

What a simple but wonderful truth!

If things haven't turned out the way you wanted them

to so far, don't worry. You can change your path starting now, because *everything is still to be done.*

If you have already discovered what you want, but don't know how to achieve it, that's okay. If you are on the trail of your ikigai, as you go along, life will show you the paths that will lead you to your goal. *Everything is still to be done* and you just need to hold on to your purpose for things to happen.

Even if you still have no idea what you want to do with your life, don't panic! Accept that *everything is still to be done* and your ikigai will eventually become clear.

This book is only the beginning for you. Think of it as a toolbox filled with the tools to help you shape your own ideas and plans to help you find your reason for being.

Now, with everything you have learned, follow your ikigai in a life full of adventures and discoveries.

Acknowledgments

To Joana Costa Knufinke, a great friend and the first editor who had blind faith in this international project.

To Anna Casals and Patrizia Campana, for pampering the edition in our country and bringing the wisdom of ikigai to families, children, and youngsters.

To Sandra Bruna and her team, for helping share ikigai all over the world.

To all the editors who have published us in nearly sixty languages, for making such a necessary concept enlighten a new era, especially for the younger ones.

To Oprah Winfrey, Marie Kondo, Mihály Csíkszentmihályi, Chris Evans, and the other celebrities who have praised our book on their social networks and made the general public aware of it.

To the wise Yoshiaki, for having once encouraged us to travel to Ogimi to find out the secrets of the Japanese centenarians.

To all our readers and friends, for being our ikigai.

The Authors

HÉCTOR GARCÍA was born in Spain but has lived in Japan for fifteen years. A trained engineer, he worked at CERN (Switzerland) before moving to Japan. In Tokyo, he earns a living working in the Japanese office of an American multinational corporation. He writes the blog www.kirainet.com, which has won several awards, has been a yardstick in the blogosphere for sixteen years, and gave rise to the bestseller *A Geek in Japan*.

FRANCESC MIRALLES is a multi-award-winning author who has written numerous successful books. Born in Barcelona, he graduated with a degree in German philology and has worked as an editor, journalist, and art therapist. These days, he gives talks all over the world and writes about psychology and spirituality in various media. His books are published all over the world. His novel *Amor en minúscula (Love in Lowercase)* has been translated into twenty-seven languages.

Together they wrote *Ikigai: The Japanese Secret to a Long and Happy Life,* which has been translated into fifty-six languages and has topped the book-selling charts in, among other countries, the UK, the USA, Holland, India, and Turkey, having sold almost two million copies. They are also the authors of *The Ikigai Journey, Forest Bathing: The Rejuvenating Practice of Shinrin Yoku,* and *The Book of Ichigo Ichie.*